LOVE IS THE KEY

...real life stories

First published in 2012 by
New Life Publishing, Luton,
Bedfordshire LU4 9HG

British Library Cataloguing in Publication Data
A catalogue record for this book is available
from the British Library

ISBN   978 1 903623 64 0

Unless otherwise stated Bible references are
from the New Jerusalem Bible, Darton, Longman
and Todd, UK (1985) and are used with permission.

Typesetting by New Life Publishing,
Luton, UK   www.goodnewsbooks.net
Printed and bound in Great Britain

LOVE IS THE KEY

...real life stories

Chris Thomas

New Life Publishing

For my mum, whose faith infuriated,
inspired, and encouraged me
and whose love, by the
grace of God, saved me.

CONTENTS

CONTENTS

INTRODUCTION

I have always loved stories. As I child I learnt to read very quickly and always had my nose in a book. Apparently, according to one of my early class teachers, I had read all the children's classics by the time I was eight. I was able to lose myself in characters and plots and story lines of all different kinds. I think because of that love I have become a storyteller and a collector of stories. These days I spend a lot of time listening to other people's stories. Sometimes when I am moved to tears, it is not always what is said that moves me but what is left unsaid which gives me space to let someone else's story touch my story.

Stories have a great deal of power in them. I guess that power is being more and more recognised in the world today and in the Church. We have theologies of story and professional story tellers, people like John Shea and Megan McKenna and William Bausch all of whom have allowed the power of story to touch the lives of those with whom they work. Spirituality is all about story. It's about our story and the story that exists between God and creation and how the two reflect one another.

Stories help us get in touch with ourselves. They act as a mirror helping us to see deeply into our hearts and minds. They help us touch the joys and the sadness that are part of all our lives. They invite us to face ourselves and often to begin to recognise our need to change. They challenge our pre-conceived ideas and inner attitudes. They bring us face to face with the stark reality of who we really are, if we have ears that are listening. They invite us to be open and to find new life and new understanding and new wisdom.

Perhaps the greatest story-teller was the historical Jesus. He told so many stories because his heart's desire was the same as that of the God that he loved, transformation. He was not interested in getting people to go to the synagogue but he was interested in deep inner change.

The Gospel stories, the Jesus stories, challenge us to let go of what we thought we knew and trust in the God who wants to work the miracle of transformation within us even amongst the most hardened of us.

Just think of some of the stories that Jesus told; the Prodigal Son, the two men who went up to the temple to pray, the landowner who paid everyone the same regardless of whether they'd worked the same amount of time. They are all stories that challenge us to see things radically differently, not a superficial change that doesn't touch our hearts and minds but deep life enhancing change. They challenge us to let go of what we thought we knew and trust in the God who wants us to become a new creation. To trust God is to open up the transforming, changing power of the spirit.

Not to be open to transformation and change has nothing to do with the Gospel. Holding on to our way of doing things, our understandings, our wisdom has nothing to do with trusting God or surrendering to God. So Jesus told stories to move us on, if we have ears that hear and eyes that see.

The stories in this book have all challenged me to reflect and pray and open myself to the spirit. They are nearly all stories from my life and some encounters that I have had. I hope they encourage you to reflect and pray and be open to where the spirit may be leading you. At the end of each chapter is a Scriptural reference for you to pray about and mull over and some questions that might aid your reflection. I hope my stories from life enable you to make connections with the story of Jesus and the stories he told and I hope they comfort you, challenge you, and move you on.

ONE

NOTHING CAN SEPARATE US FROM THE LOVE OF GOD

When I was four years old I was told that we were going on holiday. Not only were we going on holiday but we were going to France. Now that probably isn't such an earth shattering statement today but back in the early 1960's it wasn't that common, certainly not in the part of Liverpool that I came from. I lived in a part of Liverpool where if a cat had a tail it was named Lucky.

Holidays were usually days out and it always took an age to get to the place we were going and an age to get back. If we were very lucky we might stay for a few days in a boarding house in North Wales. I say lucky but you had to be out of those places very early in the morning and were not allowed back in until late in the evening. I can remember being dragged around shops in the rain and the wind and wanting nothing more than to be at home.

But we were going to France. One of my mum's best friends was a Priest and he wanted to go to Lourdes. He was going to drive through France in his old shooting brake and we were going too. It was a disaster. You can imagine six people in a shooting brake travelling all those miles in the heat.

I got lost on the Eiffel tower. I fell out of the car into a seven foot ditch full of nettles and was badly stung. My brother cut the top off his finger and to cap it all, the tent we'd borrowed had a hole in it and while it was hot and sunny during the day, at night it rained and thundered and at times we had to take refuge in the shooting brake, if we could find nowhere else to stay.

One particular day we travelled to the lovely seaside resort of La Rochelle. As soon as I saw the sea I wanted to paddle. Everybody else was exhausted with the heat and simply wanted to flop on the beach. My brother, who at the time was eleven, treated me with the disdain reserved for four year old brothers and refused to go into the sea with me; so I was on my own. As soon as I had my trunks on, I ran down the beach hardly listening to my mum who was shouting to me that they would be sitting under the White House.

After a while I got bored and decided to go back. There's only so much a four year old can do by himself but when I turned and looked up at the elegant promenade there were at least four white houses and I panicked. I ran towards one and they weren't there. Then to another and they weren't there. Back and forth, back and forth I ran.

After a few minutes I began to cry and was pretty quickly hysterical. I thought I would never see my mum and dad again. I was so frightened. I was immediately surrounded by a group of French people who were doing their best to help me but of course I couldn't understand a word they were saying and they couldn't understand me.

The noise got louder and louder and then suddenly the group was overshadowed and I looked up to see my father pushing his way through the crowd. He caught me up in his arms and my fear and anxiety were swept aside as I knew that he was there.

Despite my relationship with my father, which was very difficult, I was always able to hold onto that memory of being overshadowed by him and my fears being calmed. When God broke into my life some years later it was a memory that helped me understand something of the overshadowing of the spirit who tells us of God's incredible love for us. It also helped me to understand the power of the words from the Prophet Isaiah 'Do not be afraid, for I have redeemed you'.

Throughout our lives we are invited to enter into the mystery of love, salvation and power that is all around us if we only care to look and see. God is present. Why would God choose to be with us unless we are loved? That love encompasses all humanity, every person who has walked, who walks and who will walk the earth. We are loved. That's the revelation of Jesus.

Sadly, that offends many people. As our culture has developed it seems to have learnt to operate from a world system that wants retribution. Revenge and punishment have become second nature to us. As a student I worked in two prisons and was quite shocked when I realised that for many people who work in the prison system, rehabilitation is not a word that crosses their minds. For many, punishment is the key to the prison system and sadly the worse the humiliation the better.

That mentality can be seen all around us in society today. Litigation seems to motivate us. 'Someone has to pay' seems to be the cry in the media when a political crisis hits the headlines. We seem to want others to suffer for what they have done that we deem to be wrong. As though we were all squeaky clean and could bear to have our lives put under the microscope!

Many of us don't really like the God that Jesus reveals to us because that God affronts us. To talk of a loving God threatens and challenges much of the way society is. To cope, what most of us who say we believe have done, is to create a God that we can handle. We have made God in our image and likeness and sadly a far more narrow hardhearted version of ourselves. Because we condemn, we make God condemnatory. Because we judge, we make God judgmental. Because our love is conditional, we make God's love conditional. We make the God of Jesus into the God who trips us up and pays us back in the end.

We have taken the simple Gospel of Jesus and made it into a rewards system. If we are good then God will like us and value us. If we are not then God will send us away with a one-way ticket to hell, where we will burn for all eternity. The Bible, which for me is God's blatant, ferocious, outrageous love affair with God's people has been made into a dry, dusty, handbook full of rules to be followed.

When I was a University Chaplain I ran a survey amongst the students who practised the Christian faith. Very few of them thought that Christianity was about a relationship of love. Almost to a person they thought it was about being good, attending services, and praying for sinners. If you ask the majority of people what Christianity is about they'll say it's about morality and good behaviour and going to Church, which will get you to heaven. Is it any wonder that most people have rejected the sort of God who is merely an extension of self-righteous human beings? Is it any wonder that people do not see the Church as life-giving. The God of Jesus is not like us. The God of Jesus is pure unconditional love.

There are many people who, in the name of Christianity, have spent their lives trying to be good and worthy individuals. That's wonderful but it is not a pre-requisite for being loved by God. The very nature of God is love. In many senses, God can only love. When we realise that and begin to understand how much we're loved maybe then we will fall in love with God. It is then that our lives will change and our desire to be good and moral will spring from a relationship of love and we will become like the God we are in love with.

The Good news of the Gospel is that God wants nothing from us in return for loving us. It's really true! That has been my experience. We can go to Church every day of our lives and God will not love us any more than God already does. Everything is gift from the one who is the eternal lover. God loves all people equally, regardless of what they do or don't do.

The invitation the Gospel gives us is to fall into the arms of the living, loving, God knowing that we don't have to *be* perfect to be loved. Do not buy the lie that you have to *be* anything or do anything to be loved by God. God created you out of love and holds you in being by love and there is nothing that you can do, absolutely nothing, that will stop this God of ours loving you.

FOR REFLECTION READ AND PRAY THROUGH
ROMANS 8: 31-39

What is my image of God?

Have I ever allowed God to love me?

Dare I take the risk to open myself to love?

TWO

THE CHALLENGE TO TRUST

Many years ago I was asked to go and see a woman who was the last resident in a block of flats which had been condemned by the local council. Mary had lived in that flat for nearly fifty years and had never lived anywhere else but in the street where the block of flats was. The council wanted to re-house her in an area some ten miles away and Mary had dug her heels in, refusing to go anywhere but the area where she had grown up and with which she was so familiar.

I went to see her in her ground floor flat. As I walked down the street there were wild dogs roaming around in packs and I saw rats scurry into piles of rubbish. I arrived at the block of flats to discover that apart from Mary's flat, the rest of the block had been vandalised. The roof had been stripped and the entrance door hung on one rusty hinge. There was water everywhere. It was in a terrible state. Mary and I sat together in a room that was damp and cold as she told me how difficult it was living there and how she would move if she got the right offer. I asked her if it would not be better just to go where the council wanted her to go rather than stay where she was.

Mary was in her seventies, possibly even older, with grey hair and bright twinkling eyes and a broad infectious smile which she bestowed on me that day as she said that her faith had taught her that she wasn't a pawn in anyone's chess game. She was of value and had dignity, and then she looked at me and smiled and said 'I'll be alright, my dad will look after me.' Was that foolishness? Maybe; but as I spoke to her I had a sense that here was a woman with a real awareness of who God is and of the abiding love of her father who she really believed would be there for her. Several months later Mary got her wish and was re-housed in a flat in the next street to the one that she had lived in for so long.

I often think that the crux of the conflict between Jesus and the Scribes and the Pharisees is the claim Jesus makes that God is his loving father. It's a conflict wonderfully expressed in chapter eight of John's Gospel. Despite their history and awareness of the presence of God who had brought them out of Egypt, the Jews could not believe that God was revealing Godself to them as Father.

I suppose the question for Christians to reflect on in these days is whether or not we believe in that revelation. Many people find it difficult to believe that God is father because of their own experience. My background makes it difficult for me to trust in a loving father. My experience when thinking of my own father is of remoteness and silence and absence. I do however remember my loving mother and gentle grandmother and can understand and experience God as a loving, compassionate, caring, strong parent. Whatever image you use, not to know God in that way is hell and not life. In chapter 8 verse 59 John tells us that the Jews cannot cope with this revelation so they picked up stones to throw at him. Why is it that we are so afraid of the truth? Why is it that we seem to always want to crucify the truth?

I once read that the only sin in John's Gospel is to refuse to believe that God is father and to allow that belief to change us. The author of the book I was reading said that the consequences of that refusal are darkness, unbelief, and conflict. All the things that we find in the world today as we look at the countries that are torn apart by violence and oppression, can be seen as the result of not knowing who God is and who we are in the sight of God.

I occasionally look at what is known as 'reality television' *(which seems to be a misnomer)* and I watch both fascinated and horrified as producers and directors manipulate their so-called stars into doing things that they don't really want to do. Often the participants respond because deep within the human heart there is a cry to be noticed and valued and loved. I watch other programmes amazed as people reveal their own and their partners' infidelities with seeming indifference to the pain they have caused and I ache for them and for the potential within them. As we look at other people's lives, and maybe even our own lives, and see the devastation that lies there is it not possible that all we are looking for is peace and fulfilment. Could it not be that a

real living relationship with God is what will fulfil that
need?

So why is it that we do not open our hearts to God and allow
God to reveal the truth of who God is and who we are? That
is a huge question to ask and not one that can be answered
readily or easily but could it be that part of the reason why
we do not open our hearts to God is because the awareness
of who God is demands too much from us and we're too
frightened of what we can't control, to begin the process?
Often we don't open ourselves to the reality of God until
some crisis that we can't handle or fix demands that we fall
into the arms of God.

A relationship with God invites that we trust, that we believe,
that we hope. It demands that we let go of our need for power
and our need to be in control and let God be God.
Relationship always demands and the primary demand is
that we change. Most of us don't really want change to
happen at a foundational level and to enter into relationship
with God means that change will inevitably happen. So
rather than face the prospect of change we can continue
searching and looking for that which will fulfil us but not
demand transformation.

Jesus in chapter eight of John's Gospel tells the Scribes and
Pharisees that if they are prepared to believe in the God who
sent him, then change will happen within them. It's a natural
process. Open yourself to God and change will come, slowly

usually but occasionally more quickly. The consequence of that change is freedom, freedom from pettiness, freedom from building our own kingdoms, freedom from putting God in a box. Freedom to live as children of the father is the promise for those who are willing to let go of their own desires and respond to Jesus. Yet somehow people seem to prefer to be slaves rather than free children of God, even those of us who say we believe.

Many years ago I came across a prayer written by Charles de Foucauld who was the founder of the Little Brothers of Jesus. It was called a prayer of abandonment and it challenged me to be willing to let go and to trust and I pray it will do the same for you –

> Father, I abandon myself into your hands;
> do with me what you will.
> Whatever you may do, I thank you.
> I am ready for all, I accept all.
> Let only your will be done in me
> and in all your creatures –
> I wish no more than this, O Lord.
>
> Into your hands I commend my soul;
> I offer it to you with all the love of my heart
> for I love you, Lord, and so need to give myself,
> to surrender myself into your hands without reserve,
> and with boundless confidence
> for you are my father.

FOR PRAYER AND REFLECTION READ
JOHN 8: 13-59

Can I trust in who God is for me?

Will I open my heart to God

Do I want the freedom that comes
from the heart of God?

THREE

VOICES FROM THE PAST

Many years ago my mother was in the Legion of Mary and she was asked by the Parish Priest to go and see Mrs Malloy. Mrs Malloy was a fierce Irish woman with a reputation that went before her. Mum always said she had a pair of arms on her like a navvy and a mouth to match.

She was known to have given her husband many a hiding and her children always looked frightened and half-starved. Mum didn't want to go and see Mrs Malloy. But she was in the Legion and had to be courageous, so one day with her friend Joan she set out to see the ferocious Mrs Malloy.

She said that as she approached the house she got more and more frightened because she could hear a terrible argument going on inside. There was a lot of shouting to be heard and bangs and crashes going on behind the shabby front door. My mother tentatively knocked and nothing happened. The noise was too loud for anyone inside to hear. She knocked again, nothing happened, and then again. The door nearly came off its hinges as it was thrown open and there stood Mrs Malloy.

Mum explained who she was and where she and her friend were

from and before she had time to draw breath Mrs Malloy pulled her into the house and shut the door leaving Joan outside.

There was very little in the room that mum found herself in, with just a few boxes to sit on and a couple of cracked vases that had come from better days on the mantle piece. It was a room dominated by the presence of this fearsome Irish woman who wanted to know how mum could help her.

Mum promised to get some money for food and maybe a few sticks of furniture and when she got to the end of the visit, which wasn't quite as bad as she thought it would be, she said tentatively 'Mrs Malloy, why don't you come to Church?' Mrs Malloy looked at her and said 'I can't love, I haven't got a coat.' Mum went back to Mrs Malloy's the week after with money and some furniture and a coat.

The following Sunday, no sign of Mrs Malloy. So when Mum went to see her again she said she was sorry that she hadn't seen Mrs Malloy in Church. Mrs Malloy smiled and said she was sorry but she didn't have any shoes. The shoes came but when the following Sunday came, there was no Mrs Malloy.

This time it was because she didn't have a hat and the time after because she didn't have any gloves and then a handbag until finally Mrs Malloy looked at mum and with big tears welling out of her eyes and rolling down her face said 'I can't love, I'm not good enough.'

There are many people like Mrs Malloy, who don't feel as though they measure up to the expectations of others. There are people who live their lives hiding behind masks and playing games unable to be themselves, conscious that they always fall short.

Last year I was talking to a very successful business-woman. She was a lapsed Catholic who told me that the love of her life was fire walking. She came to see me to find out whether I would be of any use to her in helping energise her employees. The word Spirituality is often attractive to those who are searching and looking and not quite finding. When people hear that I'm involved in spirituality they often come looking to see if I can help. Initially I find them talking at quite a superficial level. I knew this wasn't about her employees.

She appeared to have it all together, was incredibly well motivated, lived in a big house, had lots of money, flash car. She was a woman who obviously got things done. In the first 10 minutes of being in my house she took 14 telephone calls on the mobile. She started to interview me to find out my skills and expertise and I listened to her but didn't answer until finally she ground to a halt and we sat in silence for a few minutes.

This incredibly well-motivated woman began to shift in her chair and her colour changed and then tears began to fall down her cheeks. Intelligent and articulate but, she told me, driven, because she doesn't feel that anything she does is good enough. The masks of success began to fall.

The illusion that she'd built about herself began to crack and we started to really talk. She shared incredibly deeply about the vulnerability and fear that she felt within and the way in which she protected herself by being hard and successful so that no-one would see. When she'd finished speaking she said to me 'so what do you think of me, now that you know?' She couldn't dare to hope that I might accept her as she really was.

Sadly we begin to hear at a very early age the voices that tell us we're no good. In response to those voices we wear masks and play games so that we can be acceptable. We hear the unwitting voice of the parent who by implication tells us we're not good enough. The voice of the teacher with his or her expectations of what it means to be acceptable. The voice of society with its understanding of what it means to be a success so that unemployed people, street people, and people with mental health problems, are written off. The voice which condemns the refugee and the asylum seeker for fear they might shake the political and economic status quo. The voice of the Church telling us that we wouldn't get to heaven unless we jumped through hoops, as though our living in heaven had nothing to do with God and everything to do with the number of rosaries we said.

We begin to believe the lie that we have to be a certain shape to fit in and be acceptable. Those voices can stop us living life which can become intolerable as we try to create a persona for ourselves that we believe will be good enough.

Whatever voices may have scarred us in the past, God can only speak one word into our lives and that is the voice of love and compassion. That is the essence of who God is and whatever unhealthy images of God you may have been fed, now is the time to let go.

I often find myself thinking about the story of the rich young man that Jesus told in Luke's Gospel. He was a man caught up with his wealth and his status. It defined him and entrapped him. Jesus cut through all of that and, we are told, looked at him and loved him. It's almost as though the young man was being challenged to believe in a love for him that wasn't dependent on what he had or on what he had created for himself but which was freely given. The challenge given was 'go and sell everything you own and follow me'. It's almost as though Jesus was saying 'Can you trust love that much that you are willing to let your guard down and accept that you are loved for yourself and not because you are rich and successful?'

The transformative journey that we are all invited to make is to know that truth that we are loved. To know it despite the ways in which we have defined ourselves, to know it despite our poor self image, to understand it as gift coming from the heart of God.

Life is about rediscovering the truth that we are fantastic, that we are unique, that we are caught up in something bigger than ourselves. Each moment is to be savoured and not endured and yet so many of us don't believe it. It's about letting go of what we have to let go of, in order to know the truth - that we are caught up in mystery and wonder if only we could see.

FOR REFLECTION READ AND PRAY
LUKE 18: 18-23

What are the voices from the past that have scarred me?

What are the masks I wear?

Who and what do I need to forgive to be free?

FOUR

EXPERIENCING JESUS

A few years on a parish retreat I met Cath who began to tell me some of her story. She had an unhappy and insecure childhood which she said was because of her father's violence. She successfully managed to hide her pain and because she was bright and intelligent went to University, got a degree and became a teacher. She married a very successful business man, had lots of money and a seemingly good lifestyle. Cath admitted that she had lived a very shallow sort of life thinking that material goods were all that mattered. She described herself as hard, arrogant, and condescending towards others and she certainly never faced the mess of her childhood.

Then suddenly life changed. She was diagnosed as having ovarian cancer with a limited prognosis. At the time she had three children all of whom were very small. Her husband couldn't cope with her illness and left her for someone else. Ill with cancer and abandoned by her husband it seemed as though her life was falling apart. Her in-laws were a great support to her. They had supported Cath when their son left and she told me that she had relied on them a great deal. I could still sense the shock she had suffered when she received a phone call saying that her beloved father in law had dropped dead.

Within a very short period everything she had known and thought of value had collapsed around her. She had to give up the family home and move in with her widowed mother. She and her three children shared a small bedroom in her mother's flat. Her children were unhappy because they had to change school. She was sick lonely and frightened. Life was a disaster. She told me that she had stopped going to Church many years earlier but one night sick from chemotherapy, she cried out to God. 'Help me. I'm a mess.' Finally she had to face her shallowness and arrogance and pride. Finally she had to admit she was insecure and frightened deep within. It was then she said that she felt a tangible touch on her hand and her very being was flooded with peace and she knew that it would be all right.

I asked Cath to tell her story to the people who gathered in the Church the next evening and she agreed. As she shared her story you could have heard a pin drop but afterwards it was amazing to discover how many of those gathered had experienced deep hardship and in that experience had encountered God. Several of them said they had thought they were mad and were too frightened to speak of their experience in case they were labeled as religious fanatics.

A couple of years ago I was working with a group of sixth formers who were looking at spirituality and prayer as a way of preparing for a pilgrimage that they were about to go on. As part of the process we watched an excerpt from the TV 'Goodnight Mr Tom'. It takes place during the Second World

War and tells the story of an encounter between a little boy an outsider because of his background, who is evacuated and sent to live in the country and the elderly man with whom he has to live. It is a fantastic story about an encounter with love that changes both of them.

It made me think as I was watching it that the Gospel is essentially about an encounter. It is an encounter with another person, an experience of love. It's an event that changes us and begins the process of transformation within us. This encounter is not about becoming more pious or more churchy but about discovering that God is real and that Christ the embodiment of God is always searching for us, always looking to break into our lives. You can call that encounter what you want, you can call it Baptism in the Spirit, you can call it conversion, you can call it being born again or an awakening. Whatever you call it, that encounter is at the heart of a life of faith. For some like Cath it happens at a particular time and place but for others it is a gradual process; but to be Christian is to have a living relationship with Jesus Christ. That means we meet him in our daily lives and he lifts us up and turns our lives upside down.

Without that relationship what seems to happen is that we turn Christianity into a moral code or philosophy. Sadly that is where so many people who number themselves amongst the professionals in the Church have found themselves. Several years ago I was invited to lead a clergy day of reflection in a diocese other than my own. At the end of the session a Priest came up to me and said 'you know you can take this Jesus stuff too far. It's enough to go to Mass on a Sunday.' The ritual had taken the place of the reality for him and for several others I have met. It's why so many people feel unable to share their experience of the Lord because of a malaise that hangs around the Church which seems to scoff at the real encounter and to limit what God can do in the lives of people.

Our God is alive and active. Jesus the Christ is risen from the dead. The spirit is at work in the lives of ordinary people and if that isn't true for you or you want to become more aware, then pray, if you haven't fallen in love with Jesus, that you do. Pray that you know in the depth of your being the overwhelming power of love that sweeps you off your feet and turns you upside down. Pray that somehow you will come to know the love that can heal the emotions, the body, and the spirit, and that can transform us *into* love. Pray that you know the love that tells you deep in your guts that God can be trusted above all else. Pray that you will know the love that gives you a sense of worth and dignity and value.

The Gospels are full of such encounters. One of my favourite stories is the encounter between Jesus and Zaccheus who met compassion, mercy and love and walked away a different person. Zaccheus was obviously a good man because despite his wealth he isn't greedy or oppressive about the poor. His poverty lay in the paucity of his relationship with God. He didn't know that he needed to meet Jesus. He was an outcast because he was a tax collector, hated by the Jews. In Luke's Gospel, Jesus is constantly inviting the poor to come up and the rich to come down. Zaccheus is the only one in Luke's Gospel who responds to that. He allows Jesus to touch his life and he does climb down, gives away his money and experiences life in that giving away.

The challenge for all of us is to be open to an encounter with Jesus. It's the challenge to know that God is real in an experiential way. It's the challenge to let that encounter change us, to be open to letting go of what we thought life was about to find something different. My prayer for myself and for those I know and love is that like Zaccheus we will have the courage to look for Jesus to hear Jesus to respond to Jesus and to find life.

FOR PRAYER AND REFLECTION READ
LUKE 19: 1-10

Do I expect God to reach into my life?

Is my relationship with God real?

Is my faith more than a moral code or philosophy?

FIVE

ENCOUNTERS THAT CHANGE US

had been University Chaplain for about five years. It was a pressurised job with lots of demands and certainly during term time not a lot of rest. I was preaching at the Sunday mass. I was aware that for the last few months I had become more irritable than usual, that often I was near tears without knowing why and that I wasn't sleeping as well as I usually did. I had got into the habit of getting into the car when I couldn't sleep and driving anywhere sometimes arriving back at the Chaplaincy at six in the morning.

This particular Sunday I was preaching holding a pencil in my hands and as I preached the pencil broke and I couldn't go on. I started to cry and had to leave Mass. I was in the throes of a deep depression. Events moved very quickly after that. My friends intervened and I found myself sitting in front of one of our Bishops who told me that I had two options. The first was that I could take control and find myself someone to help me or the Diocese would find me someone to talk to. I was not about to let others take control so on advice from someone I found myself a therapist.

I can still remember the first day that I drove to Chester to see her. I cried all the way there and nearly backed out twice turning the car round and starting for home. Somehow I arrived outside the house where she practised and eventually found myself sitting opposite a warm kindly woman. She looked at me and said 'Why have you come?' I had thought I wouldn't be able to say a word, but it poured out of my pain, anger, frustration, loneliness, and emptiness, and she listened deeply.

I left that day knowing that I had been heard and understood that something had happened to me. There was no false hope offered to me, no panacea just listening and understanding. Abigail was put into my life to help me through the darkness. Her sharing with me helped me to see things differently and make the changes that I had to make in my life. I was challenged to let go and move on and see things differently. Often she would ask the question 'where is your God in this?' I was moved to a deeper level of faith and personal awareness because of her.

Most of us will have had encounters with people that have changed our perceptions, enabled us to move on to a new stage in life and encouraged us always to trust in the presence of God. It may be our parents or friends, teachers or those we come across at a chance meeting. For me they are encounters with the risen Jesus, the one who became and becomes flesh who lived and lives among us. Encounters with the Lord will always involve change and conversion.

The Scriptures are full of such meetings with the risen Jesus. Remember John's account of breakfast on the shore and the way in which Peter had to change or Thomas' meeting with the risen Lord when he was told 'doubt no longer, but believe'. Mary of Magdala, who thought he was the gardener, and who was told by the Lord 'Do not cling to me'. Change, conversion, letting go, fresh sight, empowerment all happened as a result of those meetings.

One of my favourite encounters is the journey that Luke tells us about in the story of the road to Emmaus. Two disciples were on the way from Jerusalem to Emmaus. In the Scriptures to walk away from Jerusalem is to go the wrong way. The disciples are heading down the wrong path. They have reached the bottom of the pit, a place of real brokenness. They thought Jesus was the Messiah the one who had come to set his people free from Roman tyranny. They had been there when he'd entered Jerusalem and seen the crowds cheering and screaming his name. They had been there when their own religious leaders had betrayed him and then handed him over to the Romans who had nailed him to the tree and I think it felt for them as though they'd been nailed there as well. All their hopes and dreams had been crushed. They were running from Jerusalem wanting to get away from the possible danger and they were at the end of their tether.

The crux of their problem was the way in which they had understood Jesus. They had believed that Jesus' Messiahship was all about power and control and political overthrow. In fact it was about brokenness and pain and about the life that came from that. When things had not worked out as they thought they should, they had lost faith and hope. They hadn't understood what he meant when he talked of suffering and dying. They weren't able to recognise that it is necessary to be broken on the journey if you're going to find life.

As they walked and talked together they certainly weren't growing in their understanding. In fact, if anything, they were simply confirming each other in their cynicism and getting further and further into the mire of desolation. Only Jesus himself could open their eyes to the truth of his presence and help them understand his journey and their journey. Only Jesus himself could enable them to move from their place of darkness and emptiness to find life. That is what happens as the stranger walks alongside them and helps them to see, explaining the Scriptures to them. It's interesting that they recognised him in the breaking of the bread, a symbol of their brokenness and his. That's where they knew him.

A couple of years ago I invited Sr Helen Prejean whose story is told in the film 'Dead Man Walking' to come to Liverpool. Helen's message is one of compassion, forgiveness mercy and love as she shares her life with many people who have found themselves on Death row. It was an extraordinary evening but I think I was most moved at the end of the evening when a man whose son had been murdered many years ago and who has publicly forgiven the murderers and been to see them to offer forgiveness, fell apart during the final hymn of the evening.

He staggered towards Helen and she opened her arms to him and the two of them stood there weeping. I was fighting back my own tears at the time but have since recognised what a powerful image that encounter gave of the reality of God. The image of God that I saw that evening is a God who holds out his arms to us, holds us and weeps with us, a God who reaches out for the lost and the broken. Do not be afraid of brokenness. There you will meet God.

When they recognise the risen Jesus the two disciples on the road to Emmaus are completely changed. Suddenly their pain and their brokenness is no longer empty and worthless. They rise from the death of their old understanding of Jesus, and they rise up physically and go back to Jerusalem to tell the Good News to the others. They've moved to a different place. New life only comes through the death of the old. Resurrection only comes from death experience. If you want to experience the resurrection within you what has to die within you? What do you have to let go of?

All of us are on a journey through life. We are all faced with the changes that come from just getting older as well as the changes that happen through the living of life. Will we let the risen Jesus encounter us on that journey and will we let him move us along? Will we allow his word to guide us? Will we be open to an encounter with him that will lead us into the mystery of transformation? The choice is always ours, but not to allow the Lord to lead us into the mystery of transformation, means we remain as we are and what disciple wants to do that?

FOR PRAYER AND REFLECTION READ
LUKE 24: 13-35

Where am I going on my journey through life?

What have been my crushed hopes and dreams?

Can I recognise the risen Jesus walking with me?

SIX

EASTER DAY ALWAYS FOLLOWS GOOD FRIDAY

During a cold spell in January I was travelling home from London to Liverpool on the train. It was a rather surreal experience. The train was nearly empty because anyone with any sense was escaping the snow that was falling outside and staying indoors. Indeed I was the only person in the carriage and everything seemed silent. We trundled through empty stations where no-body was waiting and as we travelled through England it seemed to me that it was almost as though the train was cocooned in a blanket of white. The frozen silence around me became for me a symbol of the world we live in, full of so much potential and possibility and yet held in the frozen grip of sin and brokenness.

As I stared out of the window my mind was drawn to CS Lewis' book 'The lion, the witch and the wardrobe'. As a child I had always loved those stories and when I returned to them as an adult I discovered that I loved them even more. I began to think of the story of the four children, Peter, Susan, Edmund, and Lucy and their encounter with the Lion Aslan in the magical land of Narnia, a place where it is always winter, a place held in the grip of evil. Aslan's battle with evil results in his becoming powerless. He is bound and eventually killed on the great stone altar as some of the children watch from a distance. That's not the end of the story and Aslan rises again to bring freedom to Narnia, the final breaking of the power of evil as Narnia once again begins to live and breathe as in days of old.

I then began to think about the cross. For Christians it's Jesus' death on the Cross that has overcome the great battle. It's his death and resurrection that transforms the whole of creation. Jesus, the human face of God, out of love, becomes powerless and absorbs into himself the mess, transforming it and breaking its power.

I always find it very challenging that it is not the powerful way or the clever way or the strong way that God wants. It is the weak broken way of the cross that God chooses. Redemption comes through a man who is brutalised and stripped of everything. A man let down by those who said they loved him but who ran away, some pretending never to have known him. This is a man whose vulnerability and nothingness is laid bare before the world as he staggers towards Golgotha falling in his own weakness for all to see. It is only those who are in touch with their own brokenness and vulnerability who can even begin to understand it. We have to face our own pain to understand the cross and to be able to proclaim the cross otherwise it's just another philosophy. We have to know in our lives that death is the only way to life.

A few years ago I was at meeting down in the Cotswolds and while I was there I went into the Chapel to pray and my eyes were drawn to the cross on the wall. It was a roughly hewn cross but it was the figure on it that drew my attention. The figure was the gauntest most twisted broken Christ I had ever seen. I sat there looking at it for ages just trying to let it speak to me. A few hours later I was talking to someone who lived in the centre and I asked them about the cross and was told that it had been carved by a young man in the throes of depression. He'd tried to commit suicide several times and it was at his most broken and most weak that he'd carved that figure. He knew. He understood the message of the cross. It was his own weakness and brokenness that hung there.

Sadly many people don't understand the way of the cross. The world avoids pain and brokenness. We run away from that which makes us face our mortality. Most of us would rather do anything than become powerless. We build ourselves up with our own false illusions about the world and life. The way of Jesus is about facing death and trusting that through it life will come. Yet even the most ardent of believers, when all comes to all and disaster strikes, finds it difficult to trust the truth that from death will come life. St Paul seemed to understand in his reflection on the cross in the first letter to the Corinthians when he says that there is a wisdom which goes beyond human understanding. It's the wisdom of God, that life comes through death, that brokenness is the way to wholeness that the cross is the way to life. It takes a life-time and more to even begin to penetrate that wisdom. The invitation is to trust what we do not understand and which our intellect tells us is foolishness.

When I was at the University Chaplaincy in Liverpool I met a man of the road one Maundy Thursday who asked me what day it was. I told him and he asked me when Good Friday was so I explained that it was the day after. He looked at me and said 'that's my day you know.' I said nothing because I didn't really know how to respond so he took a bottle of wine out of his baggy pocket and said to me. 'It's my day because I'm crucified each day with this. I'm crucified by the people who look at me and laugh or who are disgusted by me. It's my day.' Then he slowly went on his way with the tears rolling down his cheeks.

I think about that man often because he spoke truth to me and I realised that when we look at the cross we don't just see a two thousand year old event. We see every moment when we have died within, every moment of rejection and pain that we've experienced, every moment of isolation and disappointment, every hope and dream that has been crushed and we see it all in the broken bruised body of the lamb hanging on the cross. That's how great the love of Jesus is for you and me, so great that he absorbed into himself every moment of death that has ever existed or will ever exist and loved it into wholeness.

Many years ago the late Ian Petit OSB wrote a book

called 'God is not Angry'. The cross is not some sort of appeasement to an angry God. As we look at the cross we see who God is for us, a God who pours out life for us constantly, an action that can't be defined in terms of time and space. This is God absorbing into Godself every negativity, every death, and transforming it.

In 'The lion the witch and the wardrobe' Aslan dares to believe that from his death life will come. Dare we have that sort of courage when we face the cross? Do we choose to believe that from the mess and seeming devastation of our lives God will be victorious and can we proclaim that to the world? If we can that seems to be faith to live by.

FOR PRAYER AND REFLECTION READ
1 CORINTHIANS 1: 25

Where have you known life spring from death?

Can you trust the wisdom of God?

Will you preach by your life Christ crucified?

SEVEN

CHANGE

When I was researching my family tree several years ago I discovered the story of the Barclay family and of Hilda in particular. The Barclay's were my father's cousins. Their mother, Lizzie, was my grandfather's elder sister. For some reason they fascinated me and I was determined to find out more about them. So I went to the area they had lived in and looked at their house. Then I began to knock on doors and was eventually told that the lady who lived in the house next door to the one the Barclay's lived in had lived there all her life and knew the family well. Virginia welcomed me with open arms and told me the story as she knew it. It was a sad story of a widow and her eccentric daughters some of whom had severe mental health problems. Hilda was born in 1908, the eldest of the five daughters. Her lot in life was to help her reasonably wealthy mother bring up the younger children who were very demanding. Her mother lived until 1960 and when she died Hilda refused to believe it.

The younger daughters had all left home by then and Hilda carried on doing what she'd always done when her mother was alive, washing, ironing and cooking huge meals that no-one wanted. She developed into a rather strange elderly woman who refused to accept anything that her mother wouldn't have approved of. She couldn't cope with a large house and no company and she began to decline until she was known in the area as the mad woman. Virginia had tried to help but Hilda would never let her into the house, although in later life she would accept meals handed over the adjoining wall. Hilda died in 1972 after collapsing and being taken into hospital. When Virginia went into the house, she discovered that everything was where Hilda's mother had left it when she had died and all of it was decaying, as Hilda herself had decayed.

Thank God there are very few Hilda's. Most of us accept change in our lives sometimes willingly, sometimes unwillingly but most of us drive cars, have telephones, use electricity. A hundred years ago we would not have done that. It seems to me the one area where we often refuse to accept change is the area of faith. We must do what we have always done simply because we've always done it and we like it. That is not faith, it is nostalgia.

If we want to experience God in our lives then we must be open to change. God is not in the past but in the present moment. I sometimes think we miss the moment of grace simply because we refuse to be open to change, and when we refuse to change and accept the new, we simply decay inside holding on to our religiosity but not experiencing that deep revelation of who our God is, and how much more there is to discover. We run around like headless chickens trying to appease a God we don't know and can't know because we've locked God up in the misty past and refuse to allow God to be the God of the present moment.

How many of us could answer, if we were asked the question, 'What is God doing in your life now?' For most in my tradition the thought that God could be doing anything in our lives is a foreign concept and yet Christian tradition encourages us to believe in the promptings and the movement of God's spirit in our lives. The question 'What is God doing in your life?' can only be answered if we are open to God speaking into our lives. That necessarily involves constant change within ourselves and indeed outside ourselves as well. It means that we have to let go of what we *thought* faith was about, and allow God to teach us what faith *is* about. That's a scary place to be because it means a lot of our certainties and securities have to be let go as we wait and see what God will do.

My mind is drawn to the man whose friends brought him to Jesus on a stretcher in chapter two of Mark's Gospel. When they got to the place where Jesus was there were so many people that they took him up on the roof and stripped the roof so that they could lower the stretcher down to Jesus. Can you imagine the commotion that must have been caused? Jesus stopped in full flow and the people pushing one another out of the way to avoid the stretcher and probably shouting at the man's friends for being on the roof and stopping what was happening.

I often wonder what the man himself thought? He knew that Jesus had cured the sick and obviously he had been brought with the hope that he would see Jesus and maybe be healed. I doubt that he expected to be dragged up onto the roof of the building to watch while his friends demolished it before his eyes; and then lowered him down on ropes into the middle of a room where he suddenly became the centre of attention, with all eyes fixed on him and Jesus.

Can you imagine how he must have felt when Jesus looked at him and said 'Your sins are forgiven.' This was almost blasphemy to the Jews who believed that only God could forgive sins. It's Mark showing us again who Jesus is. Try and imagine the shock horror and confusion on the face of the man who was still lying on the stretcher. He just wanted to walk. The Scribes don't understand and start to argue and pass comment about what has happened and Jesus looks at the man again and says 'to prove to you that the son of man has authority on earth to forgive sins. I order you to get up, pick up your stretcher and go off home.' Jesus doesn't get involved in their games or their theological questions. It is almost as if he looks at them and says to them 'I'm not interested in whether you have a perfect theology but I've got to show you that God cares.' And then to the man 'if God cares enough to heal your body then surely you'll be able to believe that he's forgiving your sin, and to show you that I have the power of forgiveness, I am going to give you the power to walk.'

That man in the Gospel was in a frightening place. He didn't know what Jesus was going to do but he was prepared to trust him. He was open to encountering Jesus and letting Jesus do what he wanted to do. He was prepared to let change happen in his life. If God was doing a new thing then he was ready to let it happen. This moment is the moment of grace. This moment is the moment of encounter. It's here and now that we can meet the living God if we are prepared to be open to change and newness. As Church, we cannot afford to be locked into the past if we say that we are listening to the spirit of God, because that spirit is always doing something new. As individuals, we have to be open to encounter in each and every moment, to experience a God who may say 'your sins are forgiven' but who may also say, pick up your stretcher and walk. Be open to the grace-filled, present moment and as we journey, let's pray for the courage to be like that man in Mark's Gospel; open to accepting change and willing with all our hearts to go with what God is doing.

FOR PRAYER AND REFLECTION READ
MARK CHAPTER 2: 1-12

How open to change am I?

How willing am I to let go?

How and where do I encounter God?

EIGHT

RAINBOWS

My mother had always been a great woman of faith. She wasn't just a Sunday Catholic but someone who was very involved in the Church and who had always loved God and believed that God loved her. She did all she could to share that love with others despite the difficulties she had to deal with at home. At the age of 69 Mum was struck with inoperable cancer and within eight weeks of the diagnosis she had died. After she was told that there was nothing the doctors could do, Mum decided that she wanted to go home. I was still working and trying somewhat unsuccessfully to hold things together and I panicked because I knew that Mum could not be left alone. I need not have worried. Mum's friends and my friends and my aunts rallied round and a rota was devised to make sure that Mum had twenty four hour care. After a few weeks at home Mum decided that it was time to go into a Hospice. She knew that she didn't have very long to live.

The first day that Mum spent in the Hospice I went and picked up an aunt of mine and a close friend of mum's and took them to see her. It was a filthy day driving down the motorway and I supposed it matched our mood. The rain was falling, the clouds were heavy and grey. It was very difficult to see more than ten yards in front. We didn't feel much like talking and the journey seemed interminable. When we arrived at the Hospice we went to her bedroom. It was a lovely bright room decorated very tastefully with French doors opening out into the grounds. Mum was sitting up in bed looking relaxed and comfortable and we began to talk. In the middle of the conversation Mum looked out of her window and said 'Oh look, the sign'. We looked at one another thinking that Mum was confused by the drugs she was taking or that the cancer had affected her brain. I then looked out of the window and followed the train of her eyes. In the sky was the most beautiful double rainbow.

Mum then told us that the night before, for the very first time, she had been frightened about dying. She knew that she would meet God and she did not doubt that God loved her but she was frightened about the way in which she would die. She was anxious about losing her dignity and the pain she might experience. It was late and she was alone when a Priest friend of hers called to see her. She told him of her fears and they sat and prayed together and during the prayer they asked for a sign so that Mum would have no need to be afraid. Mum loved the Scriptures and seeing that Rainbow in the sky reminded Mum of the promise in the book of Genesis that God would never desert God's people and from that moment on she was no longer afraid.

Fear seems to be so much part of the human condition. There is of course a fear that is a natural warning system that

God has put within us but there is another kind of fear that can overwhelm us and choke the life out of us. Despite how supposedly civilised we've become we never seem to be able to vanquish that sort of fear. Maybe God is one of our primary fears because God is so other than we are. God is so totally immense and beyond our control that fear is almost a natural response. Is that why so many people live in fear of God and in fear of going to hell?

Fear so easily stops us from listening. Fear stops us from trusting and how can we be a people of faith if we don't trust? Fear is at the root of much of the violence in society and causes us to hate, to blame, and to scapegoat. We live in fear of terrorism. We're anxious about asylum seekers and refugees. We worry about the influx of migrant workers. We live in fear for our children and about our future. It seems to many people that society is crashing down around their ears. At a personal level many people are afraid of not being good enough, of not measuring up to the expectation that society has of us. We are so afraid of failure, so afraid of what others will think. We're afraid to be honest with ourselves, afraid of our emotions and feelings. Sometimes we're afraid to be human in case we make a mess of it.

It's no surprise to me that in the Scriptures the Lord has to begin each encounter with his people with the same phrase, 'do not be afraid.' Over and over again the Scriptures are saying to us 'do not be frightened, trust in the God who gives you life'. Allow that God to overshadow you, overwhelm you, to catch you up in the power of love so that your fear can be calmed. I sometimes think the Bible could be summed up as an interplay between faith and fear telling us that the Good news is that the Lord has breached that fear. Maybe the reason the Gospel hasn't countered fear in the hearts of people is because we haven't proclaimed it. Indeed at times, as Church, we have encouraged people to be afraid of God; using an image of God so terrible that it controls and sublimates people rather than the truth of a God who frees humanity to live life to the full without fear.

One of the great examples in Scripture of someone who heard the call not to live in fear, is Mary. In the first chapter of Luke's Gospel we hear the story of the Annunciation. The angel Gabriel visits Mary and tells her that she is to be the mother of the Messiah. He begins to share his message and obviously Mary is afraid. So the angel utters the age old words 'do not be afraid.' And she believed it, believed that there was no need to be afraid. If God is present, why be afraid? Just as the angel said to Mary, 'Do not be afraid', so the Lord says the same to us. Mary hears the words, 'Do not be afraid,' and she allows the words to transform her life. She puts her faith completely in this God who wants her to trust and not allow fear to conquer. She obviously didn't know what it would mean for her or her child and couldn't have known where it would lead. She stands as a symbol for all of us who would journey in faith, a symbol of humanity that says 'yes' to God and allows the overshadowing of the spirit to free us from fear and to trust that God is with us.

History is full of people who have managed to respond to the Lord's word not to be afraid. Mother Teresa, too, left her comfortable convent and lived with the poor on the streets of Calcutta because she was able to listen and respond to the God who conquered her fear. Martin Luther King was able to fight for the rights of those who were discriminated against because of the power of the presence of Jesus with him. Oscar Romero gave his life for the victims of oppression in El Salvador because he had been overshadowed by the spirit of God. They trusted in the presence of the spirit. They heard deep within themselves the call, 'don't be afraid, the holy spirit will overshadow you'.

It is that same spirit that Mary experienced that can conquer our fears. Are we going be open and receptive to the overshadowing of the spirit? Are we going to hear the word of God 'do not be afraid?' Are we willing to allow the word to become flesh within us and through us so that the fear that is all around us can be dissipated? Unless we do, the world is not going to hear the words that God has whispered throughout the ages 'Do not be afraid'.

FOR PRAYER AND REFLECTION READ
LUKE 1: 26-38

What am I afraid of?

Where do I take my fears?

Can I trust God?

NINE

THE WORD IS ALIVE

Many years ago I was in the Philippines staying with my brother and his wife. For the first couple of days I lived in the lap of luxury. My every need was catered for and just for a while I became anaesthetised to the poverty and corruption that I knew plagued this beautiful country and its people. My wake up call was coming and when it did it blew my mind. One day I was taken to a shanty town built on the edge of a rubbish tip. As we approached the tip, although it was still a long way in the distance, I was aware that it seemed to be moving. As we came closer, I began to recognise shapes and figures moving on the tip; they were scavenging for what they could find to eat or to sell. When we got out of the car, I was shocked at what I saw: the shelters people lived in were made of cardboard and corrugated iron sheets. There was an open sewer running down between these dwellings. The smell and the filth almost made me gag. Nothing prepared me for the reality I was looking at, even though I had seen programmes on the television about places like this.

The people were beautiful, smiling and dignified as they crowded around us. We were taken to an area that was surrounded by screens made of rush. This was the school. The children crowded around us laughing and touching our skin. I was crying and this made them laugh even more. We must have looked like strange white people with our eyes bulging out of their sockets as we tried to take in what was assaulting us from all sides. At the back of the area were two children who didn't laugh or run to us. I still remember the shock when I was told that they would be dead by the end of the month. They had third degree malnutrition. Things had gone too far for them.

I was shattered by the experience but as we left the children I remember asking the community leader how they coped and he pulled a battered New Testament out of his pocket and said this is how we cope. I was then taken to a Bible study group. There were nearly four hundred people there, men and women who were reading the Scriptures reflecting on them and finding in them a real source of life. For those people the Word of God had power and there was an excitement about them as they told me that God was their Saviour each day.

It was the Word of God that helped them to survive and gave their lives meaning and hope. This little community living on a rubbish dump in the smog of Manila had met the power of the Word of God and lived from it. They knew that God was on the side of the little ones and they had dignity and value that no-one could take from them. Not even the bulldozers that could come at a moments notice and take away what little they had could destroy them. It was their belief in their own dignity and value that caused them to fight for rights in a world which trampled on them but it was the power of the Word which was the source of everything.

That experience has made me realise just how important it is to get in touch with our own poverty if we're ever to understand the Word of God and allow it to be a living power for us. The Bible from beginning to end is the story of a people who were broken, a people who were suffering. They were oppressed and enslaved by the Egyptians, by the Babylonians, by the Romans. The Bible, their faith story, is non-establishment literature written *by* needy, broken people *for* needy broken people.

Let us go back to my friends in the Philippines. They understood life at the bottom. They knew what it was like to have nothing and to be nothing. Since the beginning of time, most of the world has been very poor. We are not poor. Even those of us who have experienced so-called poverty in the western world don't understand what it means to be destitute as other nations do. We are some of the richest people that ever lived on this earth, although it may not always be so. I think because of that we have real difficulty allowing the bible, which is a narrative of oppression and resistance, to speak to us, because unlike those who have nothing, we're seldom in touch with our own poverty and nothingness.

The cry for redemption and liberation and salvation that the Bible screams from generation to generation can only be understood when we've been longing and waiting for those things, as the poor are longing and waiting for them.

Does that mean that the word of God can never be a living power for those of us who are relatively materially rich? Of course not! What it does mean is that we have to spend a lot of time getting in touch with our own inner state. Mother Teresa said that the spiritual poverty in the west was as bad as the material poverty elsewhere. Our riches blind us to the reality of our own poverty. For many people life is about what they possess and that somehow gives them a false security and identity. The western culture and society we live in today invites us to wear masks and play games and to make it appear as though we have it altogether.

I found myself reflecting on the story in Luke's Gospel about the Pharisee and the Publican. It's a very challenging story, which particularly faces those of us who are religious people with reality. One of the holiest people I ever met was a second cousin of mine who was dying of cancer and who'd lived a very colourful life but who'd allowed her experience to teach her about herself and about God. When I met her for the last time she was very near death but she was one of the most whole people I've ever seen. I was in a retreat centre just a few months ago and I met a woman who was a recovering alcoholic. She told her story with a humour and an honesty that was refreshing. She talked of the depths she'd sunk to and thanked God for the power she had to help her move on. That's real holiness. To know who you are, to admit who you are, and to face God with who you are.

Holy people are never those who are self-righteous, arrogant or condemnatory. Holy people are not those who think they're good because of what they do or who pride themselves on their religious practice. We all know this in theory but you know religiosity and legalism can creep up on us unawares, and we can so easily become like the Scribes and Pharisees; before we've realised it becoming the very thing we don't really want to be. Holy people are truthful, honest people. Holy people are real people. Humility and honesty are qualities of people who are filled with goodness, people who admit what they are and invite God to help them work through their needy areas.

Sadly the very people who want the power of the Word at work within them are sometimes the very ones who don't allow it to do so. We hide behind a very thin veneer of respectability, refusing to acknowledge what goes on within us and priding ourselves on our religiosity. It seems to me that what God wants is truthful, honest people who admit what they are and invite God into their poverty. People who don't admit who and what they are will never experience the saving power of God because they don't know that they need it.

To make this word a living power we have to face ourselves

and recognise our own brokenness and vulnerability. We can't run away from it. Somehow we have to recognise that we need God at the very base of who we are and join in the cry of the ancient peoples who knew their need for a Messiah. It's then that we'll see the Word of God working its miracle of transformation deep within us and bringing us life.

FOR PRAYER AND REFLECTION READ
LUKE 18: 10-14

Am I aware of my own need?

Can I be honest with God?

Will I let the word of God be a source
of power in my life?

TEN

THIS MOMENT IS ALL WE HAVE

One of my family's greatest friends was a lady called Violet. All over Liverpool, after the war, prefabs were erected to try to meet the housing shortage. Violet lived with her two dogs in one of these. She had been born in London in 1902 and when she was 18 her father moved the family up north to Liverpool because of work.

Violet managed to find a place to study nursing in Liverpool's prestigious Royal infirmary, but she contracted polio and tuberculosis. She spent many months in the very hospital where she should have been nursing, encased in an iron lung. Her illness left her severely disabled and she went through life on two sticks, with callipers on both her legs. She had a weak heart and lungs and only one functioning kidney and she nearly died on several occasions.

I think because of that she had little time for the nonsense of life. She would often say to me when I was a child, 'don't get caught up in what's not important, life is too short'. I loved her very much not least because when I was a small child she seemed to sense my fear and anxiety and was always there for me. I have fond memories of crouching with her dogs in the front of her invalid car as she drove out into the country. I had to stay hidden because no passengers were allowed in such cars. Because life was fragile for Violet she decided that every day she would do something that she'd never done before and then she would regale us with the adventure, the first time she had curry, the first time she went to a night club just to see what it was like, the first time she drove to Brighton.

Sometimes the things she did were risky for her but she did them because life was an adventure worth living and there were no half measures for her. I think she really believed that every day could be her last and so whatever the day threw at her would be embraced with a grateful heart and if it all went wrong she would laugh heartily and then look for the next adventure.

She taught me many lessons that often come back to me when the moment calls for them. The lesson she taught me most clearly was to get the most out of every moment we are given. Most of us live with a foot in the past or dreaming about the future, very few of us are seldom present to the moment we live in.

In his book the Ragamuffin Gospel Brennan Manning uses a Zen story to illustrate the point. It's the story of a monk being chased by a fierce tiger. He runs towards the cliff face and looks backwards where he sees the tiger about to spring on him. He sees a rope hanging over the edge of the cliff and it seems to be a moment of escape so he grabs the rope and climbs down the side of the cliff. As soon as he looks down he sees jagged rocks ahead of him.

When he looks back he sees the tiger waiting and then suddenly two mice appear and begin to nibble the rope. As the monk hangs between disasters he notices a strawberry growing on the side of the cliff and reaches out to take it. It's the finest strawberry he's ever had. If he's preoccupied with the cliff, which illustrates the future or the tiger, illustrating the past, he would have missed the strawberry.

In his classic book 'The Sacrament of the Present Moment' Jean-Pierre De Caussade wrote this: 'The present moment holds infinite riches beyond your wildest dreams but you will only enjoy them to the extent of your faith and love. The more a soul loves, the more it longs, the more it hopes, the more it finds. The will of God is manifest in each moment, an immense ocean which only the heart fathoms in so far as it overflows with faith, trust, and love'.

It's only an encounter with the risen Jesus that enables us to be full of love and faith and hope and so it's only an encounter with the risen Lord that can enable us to live in the moment. One of my favourite quotations in the Scriptures comes from John's Gospel. 'I came that they might have life and have it to the full.' It could be said that quotation is a reference to our going to heaven when we die or we could remember that Jesus was a Jew and that

Jews are very much a present moment people. When John has Jesus say 'I came that you might have life and have it the full', I think it is about the here and now.

So what are the characteristics of someone who has that encounter and who lives as much as possible in the present moment? They are more child-like and more playful. Have you ever watched a little child playing? There doesn't seem to be any yesterday or tomorrow; it's all about the now. The now seems to have immense possibility while yesterday is finite and tomorrow yet to come. It's no wonder Jesus took a little child and used the child as an illustration of the kingdom life because it's all about the present moment and that's where most children live. People who have had the sort of encounter that frees them to live in the moment can laugh at life because God has told them at a very deep level they are alright. Encounter frees the human heart so that we have an ease about ourselves and to be comfortable in our own skin. When you know without any shadow of doubt that you are a child of God, that your true self is only at rest when you are at one with God then you laugh more and trust more because there's a joy that bubbles up inside you.

Those who live in the moment don't have to be right, they just have to be alive and true to themselves. They don't play the power games. How sad that the Disciples never realised it and that too often we don't see it either. We live in a Church which is stained with the need for power from the grass roots to the highest eschalons of the Vatican. How sad that the Church with all its truth and beauty can seem to sell out to something less than the eternal now? The freed person, the one who is present, will be less religious and more faith-filled, more trusting in God, more aware of the presence of God within them and around them. The freed person will hold everything lightly, but for love. They will marvel at the Sistine chapel and the grandeur of God and will experience that same presence on the edge of the sea or in a busy shopping centre.

Those who live in the moment are trying to deal with their bitterness, their anger, hurts, lack of forgiveness, selfishness, self-righteousness religiosity and bigotry that lie in all our hearts, all of which stop us being Christ on the earth. You will meet someone who is open to love and who tries to let love to flow through them. You will meet someone who treats the world we live in with respect. Those who live in the moment will always be open to other-ness. They will know the truth that judging and blaming others for the state of the world, the Church or anything else never brings life. They will live at peace even with those who don't see things in quite the way they do. You will meet someone who is alive to the promptings of the spirit, the gifts and fruits of the spirit.

To live in the moment is not always a joy-filled experience. Those who do live in this way will feel the pain of others more deeply and will be more aware of their own vulnerability and the vulnerability of those around them. It can be gut-wrenching and painful but it can be liberating and it can make us feel alive in the depths of our being. Those who live in the moment will find themselves living at the level of presence. That has happened to me on very few occasions. It is more than just being a good listener, it's an entering into eternity, it's an experience of God and it is extraordinary. So dare we take the courage to leave the past where it belongs and the future where it belongs and live in the moment where our God is present?

FOR PRAYER AND REFLECTION READ
JOHN CHAPTER 10: 10

Does my past and the future dominate my thoughts?

Have I the courage to live now?

Will I trust in the grace of this minute?

ELEVEN

IT'S ONLY YOUR FEET

first met Margaret when we were both speaking at a conference in Bristol. I'd never heard of her before but was introduced at suppertime and we sat and laughed together. Margaret was originally from Barrow but was now living in Aberdeen and had a keen northern sense of humour. I thoroughly enjoyed being with her but I was not prepared for what a powerhouse this woman was. At the conference the next day I gave my talk on the power of the Scriptures and the day went on. After supper it was Margaret's turn to share with the delegates. This pint-sized woman stood up on the stage and began to share her life.

It was a brave, sad, funny, poignant story and I was held spellbound for over an hour as she walked up and down the stage telling us of where she had been. I was both crying and laughing, sometimes at the same time. She told of her childhood in Barrow and the pain of losing her father at an early age and the effect that had on her. She shared deeply of her need to be loved and some of the places that led her. She told of a child given away for adoption and the pain and the cost for both her and her daughter. Her struggle with the alcoholism that had dogged her life dominated the story. She told it all with no holds barred and with no fear of painting herself in a bad light.

Why was she a powerhouse? It was because she also told of the mercy of God who had met her in her brokenness and who had turned her around drawing all the strands of her life together even to restoring her relationship with the daughter given up for adoption. I discovered afterwards she travels all over the world telling that story and more. I don't know whether she would remember or not but at breakfast the next day she said what was for me the most challenging thought of the weekend. It was this that Margaret told me: She said 'You know, if I focused on the mess that has been my life then I would never get out of bed in the morning, but my mess can be used to draw others to God and so my life has purpose.'

As I reflect on what Margaret shared with me I find myself drawn to Simon Peter and his words in chapter five of Luke's Gospel. Jesus has just encouraged him to put out his nets for a catch. Simon, the great fisherman who knows where the fish are to be found, has humoured this strange Galilean and put out his nets for a catch not believing there was any real possibility of catching anything, barring a miracle! Of course we all know the nets are filled to bursting point and Simon's response to Jesus is, 'Leave me Lord, I'm a sinful man.' It is those words of Simon Peter that capture my attention. Sometimes it's easier to focus on how bad we are rather than to recognise that with all the mess that is our lives, we are called - chosen to proclaim the Good News.

I love the resurrection story in Mark's Gospel where Mary of Magdala meets the risen Jesus. The first thing she did after her encounter was go and tell the others that she had met the Lord and they didn't believe her. Then two more of his companions met him in the country. That's probably Mark's version of the Emmaus story typically short and to the point. They went and told the others who didn't believe them either. This is supposed to be the fantastic conclusion of the gospel and it is constant non-belief. The twelve had never really understood Jesus, each of the evangelists goes out of their way to tell us this.

Then we are told that he appeared to the eleven while they were eating. Can you imagine the shock they got? Mark tells us that he rebuked them for their lack of belief. I often think that he probably didn't say anything he just looked at them and that would have been enough. Then we get to the crux of the matter. Despite all their lack of belief and their self indulgent naval gazing he says to them 'Go out to the whole world and proclaim the good news to all creation.' I find that incredible. It does not matter that we make a mess of things. It is not a problem that we don't believe at times or even that we're sinful or needy. God can still use us.

A friend of mine was for a very long time pastor of a House Church on the South coast of England. I once listened to him preaching on the story of the washing of the feet from John's Gospel and Peter's response to it. He said, that with a little poetic licence, he could imagine Jesus looking at Peter and saying to him 'it's only your feet.' You see Peter got it completely wrong. He thought it was all about what he did and how worthy or unworthy he was.

We are so often the same; wasting time and energy thinking we're not good enough or worthy enough or moral enough, when the truth is we can never be worthy enough or moral enough or good enough for God to love us. It's God's love and mercy and free gift in Jesus and nothing to do with us at all. We can't earn love and forgiveness and mercy. It's freely given. Your mess is not a barrier to proclaiming the kingdom, so get over it. What matters is that we get up again when we've messed up and proclaim the Good News that he's alive. We have a job to do and that job is to do what Jesus did and proclaim the Good news of a loving merciful compassionate God who gives everything for our sake.

I was reminded just recently of the words that Nelson Mandela used in his inauguration speech as president of South Africa when quoting Marianne Williamson he said 'We ask ourselves, 'who am I to be brilliant, gorgeous, talented and fabulous?' Actually, who are you not to be? You are a child of God. Your playing small doesn't serve the world. There's nothing enlightened about shrinking so that other people won't feel insecure around you.' Sometimes we can use our mess as an excuse not to get involved in proclaiming the Gospel. We create a distance between ourselves and God as a way of avoiding investing ourselves in the Gospel so, yes, we'll do our religious thing but we couldn't get involved in anything else we're not good enough or able enough or educated enough. We're too sinful, our lives are too broken. Sometimes we let ourselves be overwhelmed by self pity, it's the very subtle way the ego works, focusing on ourselves rather than looking outwards and hearing the call. That mentality is our problem and not God's.

If you go back to Luke Chapter 5 you will discover that Jesus completely ignores Simon's plea to leave him alone. In that lack of response to Simon's words it's as though Jesus says 'don't go there, your brokenness and mess and sinfulness are only a problem if you let them be.' Of course there is a need to acknowledge and face what goes on in our lives and there is always time for conversion and healing as we recognise where change has to take place.

That's key to growing into mature Christians but don't let the mess stop you doing the incredible things that you are called to do. 'I will make you into fishers of people', Jesus says to Simon. Pray everyday for the strength to proclaim the kingdom, to take the opportunities that we're given to bring life to someone else.

We have a job to do so don't be overwhelmed by your self. Trust that grace is enough and that God is comfortable with sinful broken people and let's get on with what we're called to do.

FOR PRAYER AND REFLECTION READ
LUKE CHAPTER 5: 1-11

Do I hear the call to be good news for the world?

Do I let my brokenness and mess get in the way?

Can I resolve to keep standing up?

TWELVE

FOOTWASHERS

I once heard the story of a man who suffered terribly in one of the Japanese Prison of war camps during the Second World War. When he was eventually released from the camp at the end of the war he was skin and bone and had developed huge gangrenous sores all over his body. He was taken to a hospital where he lay for many weeks moving in and out of consciousness. During this time he was vaguely aware of a figure in white bathing him and changing the bandages on his wounds and he was aware of a phrase being repeated as this was taking place, 'All for Jesus'.

When the man fully recovered consciousness he discovered that the shadowy ethereal figure he had been aware of during his illness was real flesh and blood. She was an elderly nun who went far beyond the call of duty in working with those in the hospital. She would sit during the night holding the hands of the dying and comforting those who were tormented with nightmares, as well as doing her normal duties.

When the man was finally up and about he walked in the grounds of the hospital and found a queue of hungry children being fed by the sister in white. Wherever she was and whoever she was with, whatever she was doing, the phrase 'all for Jesus' was never far from her lips.

When that man left the hospital he became a Christian because of the witness of that woman's life. I am sure that clever theological arguments will never convince anyone of who Jesus is. I'm convinced that doctrinal purity will change no one's life. Only by loving compassionate service will anyone be encouraged to explore who Jesus is. It is the way that we live our lives that matters and it is the effect our lives have on people that makes them ask questions.

Each year when our 'Journey in Faith' group met in the Parish where I lived and worked I was always amazed at the witness of people's lives that had drawn others to come along. In answer to the question 'why have you come?' people would talk about their neighbours or their partners or their in-laws and the effect those people had on their lives. It's the lived experience of faith, not necessarily whether we know the teaching of the Church or can quote the Scriptures, that touches people's hearts.

One of the greatest witnesses to the Gospel was a woman who lived in inner city Liverpool. She had a little more money than others who lived around her and her whole life was spent looking after others. Her home was open to anyone who had a problem. People who were struggling because of unemployment or bereavement would often find envelopes stuffed with cash pushed through their letter boxes. She couldn't quote the latest Church document or the Scriptures by heart but she lived the reality of the Christian life and when asked why she did what she did, the response was simple; 'It's what I'm here for, love'.

John the Baptist makes his last appearance in John's Gospel in chapter 3 where he bears witness to the reality of Jesus. He is a witness because he is in relationship with the Lord, because he has discovered who Jesus is and that relationship has changed his whole life. The author of the Gospel finishes the passage with an invitation to believe in Jesus and to know eternal life. It's obvious from the Gospels that to believe is much more than just head knowledge.

That belief is about everything that we are; heart, mind, body, soul. It's about our relationship with a living God being the very bed-rock of our lives. That relationship then has an impact on our connectedness to every other created reality. If our relationship with the Lord is real and not just pie-in-the-sky devotion then we will be challenged to love the world and everything in it.

Richard Rohr the American Franciscan said in one of his daily reflections 'Once you are reconnected and realigned with God it is no longer a disenchanted universe, as it is for most post-modern people. If people had experienced the soul of the earth, we could never have poured chemicals and pollutants into the rivers the way we did for the past one hundred years. We could never have filled the world with trash and garbage.' It's very challenging to know that we are called to love and respect the very creation we live in especially when we look at how we have abused the creation and its creatures. Look at what we have done to the Amazon Rain Forests and the ways in which we have traumatised the natural equilibrium of the planet.

That connectedness brings into question the way we treat our brothers and sisters. For years I have attended a conference where there is great love for the Blessed Sacrament. People drop to their knees as the Lord is brought across the fields but the question that crosses my mind as I see this happening is whether or not we have the same love and respect for the people we see every day. It is the same Lord who is present within them. Would we drop on our knees in front of one another? If we are growing in awareness of the presence of God in our brothers and sisters then how can we stand by while they suffer in Africa or are torn apart by violence in Iraq or Afghanistan? It asks us to reflect on our attitude to asylum seekers and refugees. It invites us to ask questions about the way in which Osama Bin Laden, Colonel Gadaffi, and Sadaam Hussein were treated. These are huge questions and uncomfortable ones.

That connectedness begs questions about where we shop. Are we always looking for the cheapest bargain rather than considering the conditions of those who produce our bargains and campaigning for fair wages and conditions for them. It invites us to reflect on how we vote. Is our vote only used for our good or when we consider who and what we vote for are we thinking of the common good. How do we decide the way in which we spend our money?

Our belief in Jesus is meant to bring real life to ourselves and to others and that's why our witness has to be effective. The invitation is to live lives that let others know that the Lord is present. I think the truth is that it's only in his power that we can do that. We can't do it in our own strength. In Luke's Gospel Jesus stood up in the synagogue in Nazareth and said 'The spirit of the Lord has been given to me.' If Jesus needed the spirit to empower him to witness to the love of God, so too we need that same spirit to empower us. It's only in his power that we can share in his mission to bring good news to the poor and help the blind to see, the lame to walk and the dead be raised to life. It is only in his power that we can be witnesses.

One of the challenges of the Gospel is to recognise that it really is the fruit of our lives that matters. In biblical language it is by our willingness to get down on our knees and wash the feet of those who are hungry and thirsty and those on the fringes of society, that others will experience the presence of our risen Lord. It's by our care for the widow and the orphan that people will hear deep within themselves the Good News of who Jesus is. Will that be easy? Of course not. Our motivation will be questioned. We will be misunderstood. At times we might be ridiculed and even

persecuted but we are called to be people who are alive
with the love of God. We are invited to be vessels through
which that love can flow into the world. That's our vocation,
so let us pray daily for the courage and the strength of the
Spirit to live out our vocation to be witnesses to the abiding
love of God.

FOR PRAYER AND REFLECTION READ
LUKE 4: 16-30

Is my life lived for myself?

Do I hear the call to live for others?

Will I be willing for my life to be used?

THIRTEEN

CONVERTED FOR LOVE

I once sat and watched a mime artist named Steve Murray perform a piece called 'My Father's Chair'. As I watched the tears poured down my face. I think it moved me so much because it was an experience that was not dissimilar to my own and I found myself thinking back to my childhood, which was not easy. My father was alcoholic and a deeply unhappy man whose frustrations were taken out on his family with long periods of silence and outbursts of temper. At best my Dad seemed to be indifferent towards me. I don't remember ever being called by name or having him hold me, other than on one occasion that I was lost. I was a very sensitive child and I loved him very much and I think I hurt more because of that. I did what most of us do when we hurt inside I put the barriers up and I eventually became both an argumentative and sullen teenager. I trusted very few people and God was an irrelevance if God existed at all.

I had stopped going to Church when I was about 13. My mum had given me permission to go to Mass in the evening at our local Church. It was the so-called youth Mass and after a couple of weeks hanging around the porch, I drifted away to the local park to play football. It was only discovered that I wasn't attending Mass after about eighteen months when I came home one Sunday evening and my mum asked me 'Who said Mass?' My response was quick, 'Fr Bonner,' I said. 'Really,' replied my mum with one eyebrow raised 'how strange, he died this afternoon.' After that I went back to the dark recesses of the porch just so I wouldn't be caught again.

From the age of six until I was eighteen I was a fanatical Liverpool fan. I travelled to home games and away games. I had a season ticket for the Kop paid for by an Antiques dealer whose mother in law was a friend of my mother. I worked for Alan as a 'van lad' for two evenings a week and on Saturday morning and my wages were my season ticket. I suppose I lived for football. Bill Shankly and then Bob Paisley were my heroes. Just days before my 15th birthday Liverpool's home game with Birmingham City was cancelled and I was like a bear with a sore head. My mum, without telling me what I was going to, asked me to go out with her and the miracle was that I went. We had an old banger of a car, so we left our house and went to pick up another couple who, within seconds, I decided were crazy. Their conversation was punctuated with 'Praise God' and 'alleluia' What on earth had I let myself in for? Despite their best efforts to draw me out, I hardly spoke on the journey.

I had been taken to what was called a day of renewal. I had absolutely no idea what Charismatic Renewal was about. This was 1975 and renewal was sweeping across this country affecting thousands of people. I hardly knew what Church was, let alone what was happening here. We went into a hall where there were about five hundred people gathered. They were clapping and dancing and singing and I just wanted to get out. I thought the people were mad but I couldn't leave because my mum was standing next to me and I couldn't squeeze past her even if she would have let me. There was no way that she would have let me anyway; I got the feeling that she had decided this was her chance. Eventually it all quietened down and people sat. A man got up and began to talk about Jesus in a way I'd never heard before.

I listened to him and I knew that I wanted to know Jesus the way he did. I'd been at a Catholic School all my life but had never heard the Lord spoken about in this way. Everybody stood up and I stood up with them thinking about this man and what he had said. I think in my heart I was standing with a desire to know Jesus like that man when I was suddenly filled with a red hot flush of pins and needles and then began to cry. It was an experience that lasted about ten minutes. I found an unintelligible language bubbling up within me and in the depth of my being I felt at peace. When the experience began to pass I was left with was an awareness that I was loved by a God who was present, not up in the clouds but with me. Nothing I had done and nothing I was going to do in the future would change that. It was as though the scales had been taken off my eyes and I could see. It was a moment of grace that is an eternal moment. Whenever we glimpse the evercoming God, we stand in the grace of God.

The spirit had begun to unlock within me the capacity that is God-given, to know the power of love deep within us and all around us. Every day is an invitation to see again the truth of the presence of God. Every day is an invitation to plug into the eternal moment of grace. If you haven't asked the spirit to unlock within you your potential to grow into the mystery of 'God with us' then do it, because it brings life you can never imagine in your wildest dreams. Ask God to unlock within you the power of the spirit so that you can see more clearly the God who is everywhere. Wherever my journey has taken me since then, the truth has never left me that God is present. When you know that it changes your life. Even when many years later I became ill with depression and ended up having a lot of therapy, I knew that God was there, in it all. I don't believe that we all have to go through the sort of experience that I did, but I do think we are all called to conversion whether our awakening is a process or can be traced back to an isolated event.

Whenever I think of that day in Warrington, I am reminded of Paul's conversion on the road to Damascus. If you look at the letters of St Paul you'll discover just how important his conversion experience was for him. Paul was a member of the temple police, delegated to destroy the Christians, which he did with great commitment. Then his Damascus Road experience happened. Paul met the risen Jesus and more than anything else he became aware that despite the fact that he was a murderer and a bigot who had got it all wrong, he was loved by God. Eventually he returned to Damascus a transformed man. Real conversion changes the way people see things and do things. It turns the world upside down constantly. Paul's experience and subsequent change leaves us with a real question to consider. Have we really been converted? Do we see things in a totally different way or do we simply believe what everyone else believes but shroud it in Religious language?

How can we tell if we've been converted or are being converted? Maybe some of the points to follow might be an indication. Converted people know that God is present with us. Conversion leads you to the truth that God is everywhere and therefore everything is held in awe. Converted people don't need to protect themselves because they've given themselves away. There is no self image to protect. Paul says it wonderfully in his letter to the Galatians when he writes 'I live, no longer I, but Christ who lives in me'. Converted people know that they're not worthy and yet at the same time have a worthiness that can't be gained or lost because we are sons and daughters of God. Converted people know that everything is a miracle. After conversion the hand of God is seen in everything that happens.

When I was reflecting on some of those points I began to realise yet again that we're called to conversion every day because none of us have ever arrived. We all need to experience transformation in so many ways. The Good News is that we're not alone on the journey. God is with us and will give us all we need to daily become converted people.

FOR PRAYER AND REFLECTION READ
ACTS 9: 1-19

Is my experience of life converting me daily?

Where am I growing and changing?

How does my 'conversion' challenge me?

FOURTEEN

BLINDNESS OF THE HEART

When I was University Chaplain in Liverpool, our building was a drop-in centre for students. Our building was right next to the Cathedral and we used to get a lot of the street people wandering in looking for warmth and shelter. Student life can be very insular and petty so the street people added a much-needed breadth to life and inspired several of the students to work in night shelters round the city.

One of the men who came regularly into the building was Tony. Tony was an alcoholic, a big genial Irish man with a sad tale to tell of rejection and abuse which had led him onto the streets. He used to come into our building and sleep all day because he was frightened to sleep at night in case he was beaten up and robbed of the little he had. One day he walked shakily into the building at about 5pm and went into the toilet. After about ten minutes I followed him to find him slumped in the corner of the toilet. He was semi conscious and seemed delirious and confused.

I called my assistant, Nicky, and went for a blanket and a pillow and then phoned for an ambulance. The ambulance people refused to come because Tony lived on the streets and was an alcoholic. They suggested we ring the police, which I did. When I went back to the toilets my assistant and I made Tony as comfortable as we could and then we sat with him. The police arrived and tried to bully Tony into standing up. He couldn't do it and in the end was crying so I asked the police to leave. They went into the lounge and waited. I sat down next to Tony and Nicky and I held his hands. He looked at us both and smiled and then lapsed into unconsciousness. I went out and told the police who had the grace to look embarrassed and then we sat with Tony until paramedics arrived and he was taken to hospital. We followed him to the hospital where he was taken into casualty. The doctors said that he was in heart failure and that all his major organs were closing down. They told us that they would do what they could to make him comfortable. After a while Tony opened his eyes and smiled at us and then he was gone

After Tony had died my assistant sat with the tears pouring down her face and then as we left the hospital and we were alone she looked at me and said 'I've just seen Jesus.' It was for me a Gospel moment, a moment when I glimpsed the truth of the presence of God with us. It was like a flash of light that here in this broken battered body of a vulnerable sad man was the presence of God and it took a 21 year old non-practising 'new ager' to show me.

One of the major themes in John's Gospel is that of blindness and sight. Throughout his writing John invites us to look beyond what we see with our physical eyes and recognise the presence of God. John invites us through Jesus to see this God who has chosen to be intimately involved with all of the created order so much so that every aspect of this world is as Gerald Manley Hopkins says 'Charged with the grandeur of God'. It was Daniel O'Leary who wrote in his book 'Begin With the Heart': 'With imagination you don't have to travel far to find God; only notice things, the finite and the infinite live in the same place.'

There is no division between the sacred and the secular. Jesus has shown us that God is in it all and therefore everything is made holy by the presence of God. The challenge is to look at everything and everybody with fresh eyes and see the presence of the living Lord. I'm beginning to become aware that our very lives are gifted by God, that our very lives are graced by God's presence. If we want to meet God and to experience God then we have to enter deeply into the mystery of the world we live in and the people we live with, because that's where we'll find God.

St Ignatius of Loyola was convinced that in every moment of every day God is communicating with us and revealing Godself to us, in the touch of a child or the smile of another person, when someone listens to us, when we have a story to tell. God is making Godself known when someone holds us as we cry, in the moments of laughter and deep sorrow, in our care for another person in their illness, as we look at the trees and the sky somehow God is in the very air we breathe. It's about becoming aware and the entering into the mystery of presence.

It happened to me once in that slum village on the side of a rubbish dump in the Philippines that I've already written about. As I looked into the eyes of those two children dying from malnutrition I experienced a freedom from myself and my concerns, my ego, an experience I describe in chapter 9 of this book. All that mattered was those two children, and I was alive with a passion for Justice for the children and those like them. Another time it happened to me was in a hospice as I sat holding my mother's hand as she lay dying and I was a wreck emotionally. It seemed like time stood still as I learnt what it was like to be present to another human being and to be wrung out and yet aware in a way that I had never been aware before or since. In both of those experiences I was profoundly aware of the presence of God.

One of the truths in the Scriptures is that God is everywhere, not just in some things but everywhere. Sadly our eyes are blinded by bitterness and cynicism, by hurt and frustration, by lack of forgiveness and painful memories, so that we can't see that God is with us. If we're going to be honest, those things are within all of us. Blindness of the heart is far more damaging than physical blindness because it stops us growing and finding life and more often than not it's those who think they can see, who can't see at all. It's the truth we find in Chapter nine of John's Gospel in the story of the blind man healed by Jesus. The Scribes and Pharisees thought they'd got it all together. They had their nice neat religious package and anything that challenged it was for them beyond the pale. They weren't able to see the God who was present in all things. They weren't able to see God in Jesus or if they could they weren't prepared to admit it, nor were they able to see the work of God in the life of a little blind man who was outside the boundaries of orthodox Judaism.

The danger with all religious people is that we can become blind within. We can have our neat little package but not be open to the presence of God. We can go to Mass every day and know everything the church teaches and be blind to the presence of God in our brothers and sisters. We can be so caught up in our own self-righteousness and limited vision that we close ourselves off from the God who is in people of all faiths and no faith.

How do you know if you're spiritually blind? It seems to me you can tell by how open you are to others and to discovering and meeting the God within them. Or do you simply close yourself off from people who don't fit in to your neat little understanding. If we're going to be honest we all do it. We put such pride on being right and it blinds us to the presence of God in others.

You know the truth is that God is either present or not present. God can never be partially present; in some things and not in others. That's never been Christian truth. God has entered into the human condition and is present and our role in the world is to recognise that presence and name it and affirm it. Let's pray for an end to blindness and a new openness to seeking the presence of God.

FOR PRAYER AND REFLECTION READ
JOHN CHAPTER 9: 1-49

Where does my blindness lie?

Do I want to see?

Where would real sight lead me?

FIFTEEN

FOLLOW ME

In 1944 my auntie May died in a sanatorium from tuberculosis. She was just twenty three. I am told that May had always been the life and soul of the party, full of energy and laughter. As a child she had an enquiring mind and was always interested in everything around her. It was no surprise when at the age of eleven she passed the scholarship and won a place at a Grammar School for girls run by the Faithful Companions of Jesus.

She blossomed while she was there and had wild thoughts of becoming a teacher. No-one that she knew had ever had such high aspirations. May was unable to continue her education because my grandparents didn't have the money to put her through college. When it was my mum's turn to go to the Grammar School my grandparents couldn't afford the uniform and so our family ambitions went the way of all things. May was never a person to let adversity get her down and so she went to work in the local post office where she was known as little Miss Lively.

She started coughing two years before she died and she did nothing about it. She asked one of her friends whether or not she should go to the doctor and he said it would pass. That was a burden he would carry until his dying day. He told her that life was too full and she, May, was too free to be worrying about matters of health. When she died it was very difficult for my mum and her brother, Bob, because the three siblings had been incredibly close. They were all born within four years and shared the same friends and the same interests. They were always together playing tennis, out walking and meeting in their friends' houses. My mum said to me that when May died it was like having a limb amputated. If it was hard for my mum and for Bob, it was even harder for my grandparents. Mum said that her mother would often say that the pain of May's death was the cross that she would carry for the rest of her life. Nana cried every day for May until she herself died some twenty years later.

I suppose many of us have experiences in our lives that we call the cross. It may be illness or bereavement or some sort of difficulty that we have to cope with. It can be a comfort to think of it as the cross and I know my nana would talk about sharing the pain of Calvary. It seemed to bring her a little peace and strength to carry on. I would not want to minimise those very painful burdens that we carry around but there's a very real sense in which the gospel writers see the cross as something much wider and bigger than simply the pain and difficulty that we as individuals have to face in life.

So what is it about for those of us who say we follow Jesus?

What does Jesus really mean when he says take up your cross daily and follow me? Primarily it is a reminder to us that following the Gospel way will always involve some suffering. We cannot avoid it. At times we will be rejected and misunderstood. There will be some who treat us as though we are crazy people who don't understand the real world. While the cross encompasses the pain and the suffering we have to face in life and how we deal with it, it has much more to do with being witnesses to the Jesus way.

If you and I take on the values of love and compassion and begin to see every individual as a unique creation of God then we will begin to suffer because it will put us on the side of those who have no voice. It means we have to stand on the side of those most rejected by society, the asylum seeker, the refugee, the outcast, the aids sufferer, those who live on the edges. That will always cause tension because to be on the side of the little ones is to stand against those who have power or those who are frightened of losing what they think they have. That conflict and the suffering and rejection that can come from it, is the cross.

If we begin to really live by the Gospel values of forgiveness and mercy and peace and understanding and acceptance then it will bring us into conflict with those who preach another way of life. I remember a Youth for Christ worker who lived and worked in the town I was first appointed to when I was ordained. He lived in a very poor area and was pilloried daily because of his belief in Christ. If we begin to live simply and justly then we will begin to question the market forces that control society and allow some to starve while others live on the backs of the poor. The scorn of some and the dismissal of others, is the cross. When we refuse to enter into conversation that denigrates people and makes them appear to be less than the unique children of God that they are, we will experience a reaction as people are brought face to face with their own prejudices and don't want to change.

To take up the cross is an invitation to enter into the pain of the world, to enter into the needs of others and to help others find life in the death that they experience. It's an invitation to be on the side of the marginalised and to be willing to experience suffering and rejection because of our desire to stand for Gospel truth.

Sadly it seems that much of Western Christianity is not willing to really take up the cross and follow Jesus. It's too demanding. Despite what we say about faith making us radically different and a sign of contradiction, we live in much the same way as many of those around us, consumed by materialism and our need for power, living from a place of fear rather than a place of truth. We get caught up on the roundabout of judging and criticising and blaming others. We allow the systems of the world to be the guiding forces in our lives. We seem to have bought the values of the world and replaced a living, dynamic faith with a piety that does nothing more than make us feel good.

How can that be the Gospel of Jesus, the only way to find real life in its fullness? No, there will be conflict for those who follow the Jesus way and there will be suffering. There is the cross. Thank God faith tells us that taking up the cross is not the whole story. If it was we would die with the burdens placed on our shoulders. We could not cope. If we face the cross then somehow our suffering will be transformed into glory just as Jesus' was, somehow each and every death we have to go through will give way to life. Good Friday is always followed by Easter day. That's the promise of Jesus, that we will be filled with joy and life that nothing and no-one can take away from us. Not just in the future but in the here and now.

FOR REFLECTION AND PRAYER READ
MATTHEW 10: 38-39

Where do I see the cross in my own life?

Do I believe that death gives way to life?

Where do I stand as a witness to the cross?

SIXTEEN

TOUCHING THE UNTOUCHABLE

One of the most valuable times in my life was spent when I was a Parish Priest and as a community we opened our hearts and minds to those who found themselves excluded from respectable society. Every emotion and attitude within me was challenged as I listened to their stories and tried to respond to their needs. I had to face my own self-righteousness and my pre-conceived ideas. I had to overcome my revulsion and my selfishness. There were often occasions when I would want to shout at the people who presented themselves for food and who were difficult and uncomfortable to be with. I had to get over what other people thought of me and the looks I got when sitting with the alcoholics and the street people. They taught me so much. At times it was frustrating and thankless and at other times glorious and rewarding.

I often think of the time I spent working with people who through no real fault of their own had found themselves living on the streets or in very poor bed and breakfast accommodation. They were very brave people, at times uncomfortable to be with, but always real and honest about who they were.

I remember Patrick who wore a huge sheriff's hat and badge and carried everything he owned in his pockets. He was usually drunk but always polite. He told me that alcohol had played a part in his life from the time he was a baby when his father would put Guinness in his bottle to make him sleep.

Then there was kind, generous, laughing Pam who would give you the shirt off her back if she could. She was always looking out for the others and the first to tell me if there was a problem that one of the others had that I might be able to help with. She was eventually murdered because of her addiction.

Billy looked after his mother until she died and then slipped into alcoholism and eventually onto the streets. Billy was always sad and very near tears whenever we saw him.

Russell was a heroin addict with a sparkle in his eye and a smile always hovering around his mouth who always hoped there would be more and whose ambition was to get on a drug rehabilitation programme. He would steal in the hope of going to Prison where he thought there was a possibility of getting off heroin.

Helen, who had been a nurse, was an alcoholic and a prostitute who would sell herself to feed her habit and who often arrived at our door bruised and battered and yet would find the strength to bandage the wounds of others when she needed to.

All of those people and many like them found themselves kept out of the mainstream by addictions and unacceptable behaviour. When I reflect on those people who were obviously on the edge of society, I've realised that they are just the tip of the iceberg. There are so many more who find themselves on the edges. People who have learning difficulties or physical difficulties often feel excluded from the mainstream. People who have mental health problems often talk of being on the fringes. Those who don't have any economic power, the elderly, the sick, the infirm are treated as almost worthless and yet in the eyes of God, in truth the only eyes that matter, all are of value, all have worth.

Gustav Guttierrez, the South American liberation theologian calls Luke's Gospel 'the Gospel of the outsider', because Luke has a bias for the poor and the little ones, those for whom society has little value. You will find shepherds, lepers, Samaritans, women, tax collectors, and gentiles all playing a part in Luke's Gospel. What you discover as you read the Gospel is that Luke turns the social order upside down. He always has Jesus sitting down to share food with those who are on the edges. He has Jesus making himself ritually unclean by his mixing with those who are made ritually unclean by others. Luke's book is the most scandalising piece of writing because it says that every individual is of value and all are welcome in the heart of God; something we often pay lip service to. No-one is left out in Luke's Gospel.

Each of the evangelists has his own particular themes when presenting their unique face of Jesus. Luke is the evangelist who, in his writing, reflects most on the action of the spirit. If Luke is reflecting on the work of the spirit it's somehow in the whole area of acceptance and inclusion and understanding that Luke sees the spirit at work. It's where people are allowing compassion to touch the lives of others, it's where forgiveness is flowing and healing and reconciliation are taking place that Luke recognises the dynamic vibrant reality of the spirit of God.

That's challenging because it means that through Luke the spirit is prompting us to look at attitudes within ourselves. What is it within me that makes me exclusive rather than inclusive? Why do I experience disgust at the alcoholic on the street? How can I walk past those selling the big issue? What is it in me that makes me self-righteous and arrogant towards those who are on benefits? What is it within me that reacts to the asylum seeker and the refugee, to the street people and those with mental health issues? I think we have to face those attitudes and work through them, if we are to be authentic witnesses to the Gospel. The most antagonism I faced when working with those on the edges came from some of the people who attended Mass each day and didn't like their Mass being attended and sometimes interrupted by those who had particular needs.

I was also aware of many in our Parish community who, then and still now, responded with great generosity to those who were in need. There are many people in our Church who do go out of their way to take action on behalf of those who have no voice. We never ran out of money, food, clothes, or generous help from local doctor's nurses and chiropodists. We always found places for people in desperate need and sometimes in danger, to find a place to stay, and I will be ever grateful for all that generosity that was limitless and which moved me greatly.

I often wonder where Jesus would be found if he was physically amongst us. I think it would be with the young people who roam our estates in gangs and who think they have no value and no future, with the alcoholics and the street people who experience the degradation that comes with addictions, with those who are excluded for whatever reason. I think that Jesus would be in the midst of the Scribes and Pharisees of our day challenging and encouraging them to change and I think he would still be crucified. As Church, the body of Christ, where should we be? I have a sneaking suspicion that the spirit is prompting us to be in the midst of those in need, standing up for the little ones in our towns and our cities even when it threatens to bring our good name into disrepute, and I think it is to our shame that often we are not there.

If we are alive in the spirit as we say we are, if we are aware of the spirit's prompting, then we will want to live in the same way that Jesus lived, to walk the same paths, bringing healing and peace and forgiveness into the lives of those who are desperate. Let the spirit challenge you to become like Jesus. Let the spirit you have been given transform your attitudes and hard-heartedness so that you become a vessel of Good News for those who, for whatever reason, are the little ones living in the edges.

FOR PRAYER AND REFLECTION READ
LUKE 10: 25-37

What attitudes need to change within me?

Where do I see need?

How will I respond to what I see?

SEVENTEEN

SHEEP WITHOUT A SHEPHERD

Just recently I received a phone call from a girl who was a student when I was the University Chaplain in Liverpool. We chatted for a while and then when she put the phone down I began to think about the times that we had spent together and the conversations that would go on until one and two in the morning about God and whether or not there was a God and if there was then given the state of the world how could that God be good. We would talk about morality and faith, and Marie would always be questioning and wondering. I think I became a sounding board for her on that stage of her journey. She tried many different pathways in her search for God and whenever she tried anything new she always came to see me and we would talk about what she had done and whether or not it had helped her discover more.

I often used to wonder whether anything would ever make sense to her. It seemed as though she would be endlessly searching and wondering. Then one day I was going to meet some students for something to eat in one of the local pubs and I found Marie in our entrance hall. She was sitting with Mabel. Mabel lived rough on the streets and often came into our building. She'd been badly beaten up and was coming into the Chaplaincy for help when she collapsed and Marie and her friend had found her in the doorway. She was obviously very ill and needed medical attention. Marie's friend had gone to phone for an ambulance. I could hear her in the office trying to explain about Mabel and what had happened to her. Marie had stayed with Mabel and had covered her with a fire blanket that was handy and had put a pillow under her feet. She had washed some of the blood off Mabel's face and her hands. Marie had then taken off Mabel's shoes and socks and was washing her feet and all the time she was doing that she was singing very gently. I was mesmerised at the love this girl was showing. As I watched, I knew that Marie for all her questioning and wondering and searching had it right. She had become love for Mabel

It occurred to me quite forcibly at the time that all our theological arguments, all our soul searching, all the questions that we ask matter little to God. All that matters is love. We can be good Catholics, keeping all the rules and not have a lot of love in our hearts for the stranger and the orphan and the asylum seeker and those who live on the fringes. It seems to me that if we allow ourselves to become love we will begin to understand the ways of God. It cannot be all about being right and being moral and keeping the rules. Those can be good things but they are not the sum total of faith. Let it be about love and you will have a genuine experience of the God who is love.

I think that one of the biggest areas of conversion that each of us is called to is in the whole realm of love. One of the questions I reflect on and pray about regularly is whether or not I have been so overwhelmed by love that I have become love for a world that is hungry? I am a professional religious person. I have been a Youth Chaplain and a University Chaplain a Parish priest. I now travel around speaking at conferences and in retreat centres trying to give people opportunities to pray and reflect. I talk about love all the time. It would be so easy to leave it at the cerebral level and not ask God to melt me and mould me and use me. It would be so easy to forget to ask God to transform me into love. It is true for all of us. It can be easy to slip in to a place where we forget the heart of our faith is a God who is irrevocably in love with us and who allows that love to transform us and flow through us into the world.

We can even trick ourselves into believing that the heart of faith is about doing loving things. I wouldn't want to decry that. It is fantastic when we do those things but to do loving things is only part of the call. We can do very loving things without actually loving. That is not bad it is just not enough. Mother Teresa once said that when we do loving things we are still one step removed from the heart of the Gospel because the Gospel invites us to 'become', so that love flows through us. To become love is to be so converted and transformed that love simply flows from that hidden well that bubbles up inside us and loving actions become the only response that we can give.

There is a danger that we get so caught up with going to mass and saying our prayers and doing what we think is the right thing to do that we forget to ask to be filled with love. Paul tells us along with faith and hope love is all that will last and everything else will pass away. I am convinced that it is only by becoming love that we will in gospel language 'bear fruit, fruit that will last.'

Every time I read the papers or watch the television I'm always saddened by the stories I'm faced with. Not a page in the paper goes by without stories of wars, violence, rapes, people using one another, victims of racism sexism and all sorts of prejudices telling their stories. Our television screens are full of the horrors of Iraq, Afghanistan, Syria, Palestine, Israel. It paints a gloomy picture and it is easy to get depressed and lose heart and start to believe that the world is a terrible place and the people in it are hell-bent on destruction. I am sure that picture is no more horrendous than at any other time in the history of the world. It simply shows us very clearly that people are in desperate need, searching for peace and fulfilment but usually living in fear and reacting to others out of fear. I am sure that most people in the world are not evil; they are simply lost, and people who are lost and hurt and broken, damage themselves and others.

In chapter 9 verse 36 of his Gospel Matthew describes most people as being like sheep without a shepherd. Have you ever seen sheep without a shepherd? They run around in complete confusion bumping into one another and hurting both themselves and others. It's a good analogy for the perennial state of the world. Matthew goes on to tell us that Jesus felt sorry for the people and began to teach them. It is obvious that Jesus saw the potential in the people he spoke to. He saw them as a rich harvest that had to be gathered before it went to seed. He compares the people to full ears of wheat to be reaped or ripe grapes to be gathered. There is always hope for our world and for us. There is always potential and possibility because of the presence of Jesus and his love. That love needs to be shared to let people know that real love is the answer to their searching. I would invite you to take some time every day praying that you become love in a world that is struggling to understand what real love is about. Pray that you become love for the sake of the world and be a real sign of contradiction as love flows freely from your transformed heart.

FOR PRAYER AND REFLECTION READ
MATTHEW 9: 35-37

Is my heart becoming love?

How do I see the world and people in it?

Will I give my life for love?

EIGHTEEN

BECOME WHAT YOU HAVE RECEIVED

A few years ago I was on holiday in Madrid, which is a wonderfully cosmopolitan city with people of all sorts of persuasions adding to its vibrancy and colour. Late one night my friend and I were crossing the city to go back to the hotel we were staying in. It was about two o'clock in the morning. We stopped to get a taxi in a square that was full of people who were obviously homeless. Some were begging and some didn't even have the energy to do that. They simply sat clutching their pathetic bundles. As we stood in the taxi queue a mini bus pulled up and several young people jumped out of it and they began to move around the square sitting next to the homeless people and producing food and water out of their bags for them. I watched one young girl who was very close to us. She sat down in a doorway next to a bundle of old newspapers and began to talk.

Eventually the newspapers began to move and out of the pile emerged an old woman. She looked about ninety but was probably only fifty. As they talked, the woman took off her shoes and socks. Her feet were in a terrible state, bleeding and ulcerated and the girl opened one of the flasks she had with her and poured water over the woman's feet and very tenderly dried the woman's feet on her skirt. She then produced some ointment and rubbed it into her feet. Finally she took some new socks from her bag and then food and drink for the woman. It was like watching a Gospel passage in action.

I remembered the story of Simon the Pharisee and the woman who burst into the room and wept over the feet of Jesus. It was such a powerful moment. Here was this woman, rejected by the vast majority of society meeting in that young girl compassion and tenderness. It was for me a real image of who God is, and it challenged me yet again to realise that this God who is love, is at home with dirt and mess and that God is in the midst of brokenness and vulnerability. It showed me again that God is there in the darkness of sin and in the pain of life. If we have any truth to proclaim to the world, it means we have to be like the God we say we love, which means as Church we have to be with the lost and the broken. Somehow we have to be there in the mess that is often people's lives.

I remember one of the women who was very involved in the homeless project running in the Parish, being faced at the end of a long hard day with about twenty people needing food. There was nothing left and so she stood in the middle of the room and said 'Lord these are your people and they're hungry. What do we do?' Virtually as she finished the prayer the door bell went and one of the local bakers stood there with a tray full of bread and pies freshly made. He'd heard of what we were doing and thought he might be able to help.

I've begun to realise that the power of the Gospel is to be seen in love, not in the muscular force of which Christianity has been the perpetrator over the centuries and which finds its roots deep within our humanity and our need for power over others, trying to force people to think and do what we think and do. It is in the power of the Spirit, impelling and transforming us to be a like a young girl who got up in the middle of the night in Madrid to wash the feet of an old woman in a square. The power that would prompt a baker to bring bread and pies to some hungry people. The same power that filled Jesus and drove him to love in the way that he experienced God loving, in the power of the spirit. That way of living is costly. It demands that we let go of our own desires and wants and needs and be filled with love. It demands that we enter into the process of deep transformation which the Gospel calls us to, a transformation that frees us from the concerns of the ego and allows love and power to flow through us.

One of my favourite stories in the Acts of the Apostles is the story of Simon the magician. Simon was by no means an unusual type in the ancient world. There were many astrologers and soothsayers and magicians who had a great influence and made a comfortable living. Simon was impressed with the visible effects of the laying on of hands and he tried to buy the ability to do what the apostles could do. He wasn't interested in bringing the Holy Spirit to others so much as in the power and prestige it would bring to himself.

How many of us are the same? Into the ways of faith for what we can get out of it because it makes us feel good and fulfils our need for being self-righteous, gives us somewhere to exercise power rather than allowing the spirit the space and the time to work through us. It's so easy to fall into the pattern of fulfilling our own need, which is simply another way of letting the ego run riot.

Is the process of transformation happening within us? Is the power of the spirit at work changing us? Is the power of the spirit freeing us so that we can become love for the world? Where in our lives are we learning how to love? They're the questions that matter. Are we inviting God every day to melt us and mould us and fill us and use us?

We celebrate Eucharist most days in our churches. There is a temptation to think that every celebration of Eucharist is an end in itself. It's not true. We are being called in every celebration to become what we have received. St Augustine way back in the 4th century said that we who are the body of Christ receive the body of Christ to become the body of Christ. What we have received we are to become so that we can feed the world with this Jesus whose love brings life. It's only love that will have an effect in the world and if you can't love, then words mean nothing.

That's why John in chapter 13 of his Gospel doesn't bother telling us what Jesus did when he took bread and wine but concentrates more on what that means. He gives us the significance of the moment, the kairos moment that we become what we receive by having Jesus wash the feet of his disciples. We're to become Jesus for the world. Eucharist was never meant to be about collecting graces so that we can get to heaven. It was never meant to be that but to fill us with the power to be like Jesus, to be disciples. So John tells us that it's about getting down on our knees and washing the feet of our brothers and sisters. It's about service and becoming the love of Christ for the world. I think that's why the Church says that the Eucharist is the source and summit of all that we do.

Where does all that leave us? We live in a world that's desperate to see and hear the power of the Gospel. It will see it in the love that flows from the transformed heart and in the love that is big enough to embrace all. It will see it in communities of people who are walking the journey together trying to be Christ for the world. It will hear it as we proclaim the Gospel of love that is alive within us.

FOR REFLECTION AND PRAYER READ
JOHN 13:1-15

Where am I being transformed?

How is the spirit empowering me?

Have I the courage to make a difference?

NINETEEN

BE RECONCILED

Most weeks I have a chat with Mark who is a Big Issue seller in a town near where I live. Mark's twenty three years of life has been a real roller coaster of a ride. He was placed in care at the age of three because of his mother's alcoholism. For several years she was allowed supervised access but Mark told me that whenever he saw his mother he was filled with rage and anger which would explode into violence.

He was placed in several foster homes but his relationship with his various foster parents always broke down. When he was fourteen he ran away from the children's home that he was living in for the first time. He was found and returned but on his ninth 'escape' he told me that no-one came looking. He managed to get himself to London where he lived on the streets and became addicted to heroin and crack cocaine.

He returned to the North of England when his best and only friend died from a heroin overdose. He described it as a wake-up call. Suddenly he knew he didn't want his life to end in the same way as that of his friend. Mark managed eventually to get himself on a methadone programme and found a small flat and his job as a Big Issue seller, and life was slowly beginning to turn around. I wouldn't like to think what this young man has seen and been exposed to in his relatively short life.

He'd never asked me what I do until the day when finally he asked me what my job was. This was after about five years of chatting and drinking coffee now and again at his pitch. So I told him I was a Catholic Priest. After a moment of silence while he got over the shock he said, 'You know, I think I could be a Christian if there was space for people like me and if it didn't mean I'd have to go to Church and be part of all the hypocrisy and fighting that goes on.'

I know that attitude towards Christianity is often about perceptions but I do sometimes look at the Christian Church and I'm saddened by the amount of wrangling and dissension that goes on between the different traditions and within them. We fight and argue about who is right and who is wrong when it's not about being right but about being open to difference. It seems to me that as Christian traditions there is a need for respect and tolerance and recognition of one another's giftedness.

As a Christian Church in this nation we are a very small minority and yet we are split into so many different groups. Each of those groups has its own way of doing things and sadly we have learnt not to trust our brothers and sisters and their giftedness. How can we ever be an effective witness to the unity that is in the heart of God with so much disagreement and conflict? At a grass-roots level we could open our doors to one another and welcome one another. At a hierarchical level maybe it is time to set aside who is right and who is wrong and do what we are called to do and serve the world together.

I know there have been huge strides in the quest for unity since the Second Vatican Council. People entered into local ecumenical covenants and pulpits were exchanged. In the 1970's much of the charismatic element of the Church was ecumenical but in recent years even that desire for unity seems to have lost its way. Much more is needed if we are not to be a counter-witness through our lack of unity.

I'm sure that if unity is to be a reality between Church traditions it has to first start within each denomination. I look at our own Catholic tradition, with all its beauty and historical depth and the ways in which the spirit has worked leading us forward, and wonder how we can spend so much time fighting about theology and rubrics and Liturgy. I wonder why as Church we can't be open with one another and enter into dialogue with one another without the risk of being silenced from above.

I look at the promise of openness and new life that sprang from the Second Vatican Council that excited and empowered so many in the 1960's and 1970's and am saddened by the way in which its power and influence seems to be diminishing, leaving huge numbers of people confused and angry. Unity within will only come with the freedom to talk and share without fear.

Many years ago when I was in the Seminary we were visited by the late Dom Helder Camara, who was then the Archbishop of Rocife in Brazil. He was a very small man in stature but a giant in the ways of faith. I will never forget him standing up in Durham Cathedral lost in the pulpit, a tiny figure in white and saying loudly and firmly 'People ask, am I left or am I right. Me, I am for Jesus.' When people look at those of us who say we are Christian do they really see the body of Christ or do they see a parody of what we are meant to be?

What does it mean to be the body of Christ? Words like unity, love, service, peace, compassion, mercy, and forgiveness immediately spring to mind. Other words like tolerance and understanding are not far behind. That translates itself into a way of life that embraces and encompasses rather than divides and separates. It has to be about forgiving the sins of the past.

As Church communities, can we not let go of the sins of our fathers and forge ahead in the paths of unity? Can we not reach out to the most disadvantaged in our society and work together to bring peace into the lives of those who are broken and hurt? As Church, can we not stand on the side of those who experience prejudice and oppression? As Church, can we not be courageous and love those who would consider themselves our enemies? Can we not learn to be the Body of Christ, so that those like Mark can look on and see a united body, and find a place inside?

For that to happen demands sharing, co-operation, humility, and service and is what it means to be the Body of Christ. The challenge we are given is to let go of the world's way of thinking about judgement, forgiveness, and love and take on the understanding of the kingdom. To be the Body of Christ and to live in the kingdom is to enter into quality relationships of love, forgiveness, and peace that brings life to ourselves and to others.

In Matthew's gospel Jesus says 'it's not those who say Lord, Lord who will enter the Kingdom of heaven but those who do the will of the Father.'(Matthew 7:21). Maybe it is time to stop arguing and fighting and do the will of God by laying aside our differences and begging forgiveness for our unwillingness to be the Body of Christ, with all that means. The third step in the alcoholics anonymous process is to hand yourself over to a higher power. For unity to be a reality, to live in the kingdom and proclaim the kingdom, we too have to hand ourselves over to the higher power. It is the work of the spirit to draw us together into one body.

The community that I am part of and pray with most weeks, holds dear the truth that none of us have it altogether but all together we have it all. It's when we live respecting our brothers and sisters in Christ and living and working with them, that people will know that the Church is the living body of Christ and that faith enables people to live differently and more fully than those who do not embrace faith.

FOR PRAYER AND REFLECTION READ
MATTHEW CHAPTER 7: 21-27

Do you have a heart for unity?

How are you challenged by others understanding?

Where can you work for unity?

TWENTY

RISKING AND TRUSTING

Every six to eight weeks I have to go to London for a meeting. As soon as the meeting is over I rush into central London to spend an hour or so browsing in my favourite bookshop. One day as I left the shop with a bag full of books I decided to go to Covent Garden. I was crossing Leicester Square and as I did so a woman passed me and I did a double take because she was obviously a man dressed as a woman.

There were people around nudging one another and looking. I caught her eye and saw how much pain there was behind the mask and how much energy and bravery it took just to walk through the crowd. I carried on walking and heard a bit of a commotion behind me. I looked round to see the person in question attempting to gather belongings together from the floor. There were a group of lads standing round laughing. They had obviously tripped her up but before I could get back to help she had managed to stuff everything into her bag and was already running towards Piccadilly Circus.

I continued on my journey toward Covent Garden. I was mulling over what I'd seen when I noticed a crowd of people ahead of me gathered round what looked like a bundle of old clothes. It turned out to be someone who was very drunk and who obviously slept rough. He was lying on the floor cursing and swearing with this group of people standing around watching. As I approached, a police van pulled up, the group dispersed, the man was lifted into the van, and life returned to normal. It made me think about how bad we are at dealing with anything that is out of the ordinary. How uneasy we are at dealing with difference.

My mother was very friendly with the Good Shepherd sisters and as a small child I was always in and out of their house in Liverpool seeing one sister or another. In the hallway of their house was a beautiful picture of the Good Shepherd leaning out over a ravine desperately trying to reach a sheep that was trapped on the ledge below. For many years we had a copy of that picture in our own home and after God found me I would often marvel at the compassion in the eyes of the shepherd and the strength in his arms but more than that, at the risk he took to rescue the sheep.

It is craziness for a shepherd to leave the sheep to look for the lost one. He stands the risk of losing them all. It makes no sense at all. God is like the shepherd who leaves all his sheep to look for the lost one. God is not about common sense. God is about love that knows no boundaries and which will go to the ends of the earth for the sake of those that are loved.

God was willing to take the risk to become one of us simply so that we might see who God is. That we might recognise compassion and mercy and forgiveness, God took the risk to break into time and history so we could see and touch and taste the reality of God. I don't believe that we've even begun to grasp the amazing love of a God who would do that. God let go of everything, power and majesty, to break into time and space. God was willing to trust that we would understand and open our hearts to the power of love in Jesus. That is an incredible risk and takes incredible trust. I cannot begin to find words to describe that love. It is too big a concept to grasp. It is too great for us. Why can we not believe in this amazing love? Why are we so afraid of it and unable to cope with it? Why do we limit it and put conditions on it? It is a free gift and it is given for you and for me. It is extraordinary.

Our God is the risk-taking God. The God who took the risk to become one of us so that we would see and understand who God is, and who in Jesus risks everything to sit down with the broken and the hurting, indeed the God who searches out what was lost. Our God is not the God of respectability and narrow moralistic preaching, but the God who searches out the lost and the lonely and the different and the broken and sets up camp with them.

If God is in the business of risking and trusting then we're invited to be the same. Disciples are to be like the master. We are to be willing to risk anything and everything for the power of love. We are to trust more in the power of love than in anything else and to take the risks that are called for in proclaiming love. For too long we have thought being a disciple was about keeping rules and regulations and fulfilling rituals. For too long we have allowed the radical call to live to be submerged by narrowness of being right. To be a disciple is to be so caught up by the power of love that has risked everything for us, that we can do no more than risk everything in response. While I believe all that to be true I look at my own life and wonder how at times I can be so far away from taking the risks that love asks of me, with its willingness to accept difference and to always walk the extra mile. I wonder what it is that makes me want to judge others and separate and divide them into different camps, good and bad. Is it so that I can look at those I saw in London and feel superior and right?

I think I have to find the courage to deal with that within myself which doesn't handle difference well and allow the Spirit of God the space and the time to deal with my hard-heartedness, ingrained attitudes, and prejudices. I am sure that I have to face my need to be right with all the negativity that carries with it. I think I certainly have to pray for the courage to stand up for those we categorise as different and proclaim their dignity as children of God even when that brings me into conflict with authority. That for me is what discipleship is all about. Deal with self, face the consequences of refusing to judge and wanting to love, whatever the cost.

My experiences in London have left me with lots of questions. How willing am I to accept those who are different to me and allow the love that is in the heart of God to touch others? What risks am I prepared to take to let the Gospel be proclaimed? Would I have the courage to sit down with those whose ways and lives are different from mine and allow the compassion and mercy of God that I have received to flow through me into their lives?

FOR REFLECTION AND PRAYER READ
LUKE 15: 4 -7

What does it mean to me to be a disciple?

How do I respond to otherness?

Am I prepared to take risks to proclaim the Gospel?

TWENTY ONE

CHOOSE LOVE

I n 1947 a family moved from bomb-torn Scotland Road to an area in Liverpool that had not been as badly damaged by the bombs. They were full of hope as they began their new life but they soon discovered that they missed the camaraderie of their old neighbourhood and their new neighbours, although nice enough, were too caught up with rebuilding their own lives to worry about how they were settling.

The Parish Priest became aware of them when he found Teresa sobbing her heart out in Church one day and she told him how lonely she felt and how hard life was. My mum was a member of the Legion of Mary and was asked by the Priest to go and visit this family and to befriend them. She did that and for the next forty-five years our family and theirs became firm friends. They were lovely people, always ready to help when ever we had a crisis and always there to celebrate with us whenever we were celebrating.

When my dad died it was John, Teresa's husband, and Ronnie, their son-in-law, who always called in to make sure Mum was all right and to do any odd jobs. When mum needed a shoulder to cry on it was to Teresa and Joan, her daughter, that she turned. When my Mother died the first people I phoned after my family were the Robinsons. I can still remember Teresa crying when I told her and saying over and over again 'My beautiful lady's gone, my beautiful lady's gone.'

Within a very short time after my mum's death, Joan had died of cancer and within a month Teresa, who was then in her eighties, was rushed into hospital. John, her husband, phoned me. 'Ma's in hospital and there's not long left' I dropped everything and rushed to the hospital. I was the only one there and I sat by her bed holding her hand. She was deeply unconscious and I was thanking her for all the support and friendship that she and her family had given us. Suddenly she opened her eyes. She looked at me with tears pouring down her cheeks and she said to me 'Did I love them enough.' I was a little confused and asked 'Who?' 'Your mum and Joan' she answered. I can still remember the relief on her face as I said 'Yes' and she closed her eyes. Within half an hour Teresa had died.

The question that Teresa asked me is the only one that really matters. Love is the core message of the Gospel. I am told that if you read the Gospels in Greek you find the word agape used over and over again. Apparently the ancient Greeks used the word to describe the immense value placed on precious stones or other articles that were considered to be of great value. When you read the Gospels you find Jesus placing valuing people higher than anything else, particularly those people who are normally rejected, knowing that in every human person is the spark of the divine. He sees through all the rubbish that we surround ourselves with and looks at the jewel which is at the core of every person.

Agape in the Gospels is a positive choice to live in a particular way. It's a choice to live believing in potential, possibility, hope, and goodness. It's to live in the world with a heart and mind that is unlocked and available. To choose Agape means there is no room in our hearts for hatred and mistrust, judgement and condemnation. It's not an emotional reaction to the world and its people but a choice as to how we view the world and how we act. It's a way of embracing the world rather than separating oneself from it. In the kingdom you reach out to those that the world rejects.

I think one of the problems we have with the word agape is that we interpret it as meaning love, which for most of us is seen as an emotion or a feeling. The agape of the Gospels, the love that permeates every encounter and every story in the gospel, isn't about feelings. It's a stance or a position that we choose. Agape love isn't a theory. It insists that we make the choice to reach out to those in our society who experience rejection from others and the judgement of others. It is a believing and a seeing and a trusting that God is present in everyone and therefore love is the only way to respond. Central to the Gospel message of love is an appreciation of difference and respect for what is other. Agape love has nothing to do with like-minded people supporting one another. If you look at the Gospels you will know that most of Jesus stories are about those who were unclean being drawn into life.

Has your heart been enlarged by the spirit of God so that agape love is at the centre of who you are no matter where that might lead you? Agape love is about choosing to believe in the presence of God in everyone and everything, regardless of who they are and what they are. It's about choosing to believe in the presence of God in me and in others. It's about holding the tension and watching and looking for goodness.

It is too easy for us to stay locked into the narrow confines of religion and make them our security, never becoming what God is calling us to be, a people who choose to love whatever the cost. It is simpler to remain closed to journeying and discovering rather than be open to the call of love. In Matthew's Gospel Jesus makes it very clear that it is our loving response to our brothers and sisters that determines how real our faith is. It is the acid test of faith. When Jesus tells the parable of the sheep and the goats he presents us with the stark question, 'Will you choose to love in even the most difficult of situations and will you choose to love the poorest of the poor?'

Christianity was never meant to become a movement where like-minded people got together and enjoyed themselves. Our faith and our belief demands that we change so deeply that we become like Jesus. Jesus, who had no time for pettiness, who had no time for illusion, who could only see the presence of God all around him and who chose to love. That choice to love meant that his life was taken from him by small-mindedness and the refusal to see. Do not let your vision of what it means to be a person of faith become small by limiting your response to love. Don't let this incredible gift of faith we have been given become so narrow that we become a parody of love. Open yourself to the gift of the spirit and let the power of God change you so much that you choose Agape love wherever that may lead, and then get excited about where the choice to love will take you.

FOR PRAYER AND REFLECTION READ
MATTHEW 25: 31-46

Will I choose love?

Will I allow my choice to lead me
into uncomfortable spaces?

Can I be like Jesus?

CONCLUSION

Just recently I was invited to go to speak at a conference in Ireland. There were about 300 people gathered, one of them was wheelchair bound. During one lunch break I managed to speak to Michael. He was just able to speak although the muscles in his throat didn't work properly and his right hand was free to move to control his wheelchair He told me that he had been paralysed in an accident which had resulted in his wife's death. As he told me the story the tears fell down his cheeks. Eventually I asked him why he thought he had survived the crash and a smile lit up his face and he said, "So that I can tell people that God is enough."

I was stunned! Here was this man hit by tragedy, his life seemingly destroyed and yet aware that he was sustained by a presence that was fulfilling him deep within. He told me that he spent much of his day in silence initially because it hurt to speak but then because the silence somehow comforted him and helped him as he worked through all that he felt about what had happened to him.

He smiled as he shared how in that silence he experienced in a very deep way the presence of God. It was obvious what it was that sustained him and filled his very being. Even though I spend time in quiet every day I felt how little I was aware of the presence of God and how often I avoid that place of deep silence where I can meet the God who lives.

God wants a personal relationship with us. God wants intimacy with us. We are invited into the very life of God, the dance of God. Whether we are aware of it or not, every moment of our existence is an encounter with God. Our experiences, and the stories they leave us with, enable us to reflect on and discover more deeply the presence of God which is within us and all around us.

Nothing in our lives is wasted. Even the painful incidents, the disappointments, the fears, the worries, can lead us more deeply into the reality of a God who is present even in the very air we breathe.

Reflecting on our stories can enable us to get in touch with the deep mystery of God. It can enable us to see and know that God is with us in every aspect of our lives, living and dying and rising in the very stuff of our existence. To reflect on our stories and begin to see opens us to a way of living that has roots in the heart of God. It lets us know the truth of Paul's words when he says, 'It's not I that live, but Christ who lives in me.' To pray through our encounters and to see in everything the presence of God, enables us to live in the sustaining, ever present power of God.

I know as I look back through my life that I have been blessed by presence and I know that I am learning more and more to look at everything with awe and wonder as the means by which God communicates with me. I don't always understand and sometimes confusion reigns within me but I have glimpsed enough to know that God is with us.

As for the stories and the encounters they continue. I hope it's not arrogant to say that the stuff of my life continues to provide me with insights into God that whet my appetite and increase my desire for more of God. I know that the place I will find God is 'on the road to Galilee' and I hope and pray that as you reflect on the journey you are on, and the people you meet, and the incidents that happen, and the stories you hear, that you too will know that God is with you.

*Further copies of this book
can be obtained from*

Goodnews Books
*Upper level
St. John's Church Complex
296 Sundon Park Road
Luton, Beds. LU3 3AL*

*www.goodnewsbooks.net
orders@goodnewsbooks.net
01582 571011*